The
Chief
Student
Affairs
Officer

ARTHUR SANDEEN

The
Chief
Student
Affairs
Officer

LEADER,
MANAGER,
MEDIATOR,
EDUCATOR

Jossey-Bass Publishers

San Francisco • Oxford • 1991

THE CHIEF STUDENT AFFAIRS OFFICER
Leader, Manager, Mediator, Educator
by Arthur Sandeen

Copyright © 1991 by: Jossey-Bass Inc., Publishers
350 Sansome Street
San Francisco, California 94104
&
Jossey-Bass Limited
Headington Hill Hall
Oxford OX3 0BW

Library of Congress Cataloging-in-Publication Data

Sandeen, Arthur, date.
    The chief student affairs officer : leader, manager, mediator,
educator / Arthur Sandeen. — 1st ed.
        p.   cm. — (Jossey-Bass higher and adult education series)
    Includes bibliographical references and index.
    ISBN 1-55542-351-5
    1. College student personnel administrators—United States.
I. Title.   II. Series.
LB2343.S26   1991
378.1'12—dc20   90-28987
                                                                          CIP

Manufactured in the United States of America

The paper in this book meets the guidelines for
permanence and durability of the Committee on
Production Guidelines for Book Longevity of
the Council on Library Resources.

JACKET DESIGN BY WILLI BAUM

FIRST EDITION

Code 9155

The Jossey-Bass
Higher and Adult
Education Series

Consulting Editor
Student Services

Ursula Delworth
UNIVERSITY OF IOWA

CONTENTS

PREFACE

"As vice president for student affairs, you will be expected to develop and institute a program that will increase the number and quality of freshmen admitted to the university, and also a program designed to improve retention of these students."

"The university will not tolerate racist or sexist acts on the part of students. It is the responsibility of the chief student affairs officer to implement policies and programs to ensure that problems of this kind do not occur."

"With the increasing enrollment of older students and the desire for the university to meet the needs of women, an extensive child-care program is mandatory. The student affairs vice president should provide the leadership to ensure that it happens."

"Relations between students and the community are increasingly strained because of excessive alcohol use and loud noise in student apartment complexes. It is the job of the student affairs leader to correct this."

"Fear is increasing among students on campus as a result of crime. This could seriously affect our enrollment. The chief student affairs officer, acting in conjunction with local law enforcement agencies, must develop a strong and comprehensive security system."

"The conflicts between certain student organizations and ethnic groups within the student body are dangerously polarizing the campus. The vice president for student affairs has the responsibility to resolve the differences and teach the students how to live together in peace."

These actual statements, made recently at various colleges and universities, reveal the universities' diverse expectations of chief student affairs officers and illustrate the complex nature of the position and its expanded leadership responsibilities.

For many years, student affairs was primarily associated with traditional programs such as student activities, housing, and student conduct, but now it includes a broad array of campus services and programs: admissions, orientation, registration, and financial aid; health services, child care, and personal counseling; campus security, multipurpose facilities, and transportation; intercollegiate athletics and recreation; career planning, placement, and academic support services; and student assessment and retention programs.

The role of the chief student affairs officer — most commonly called vice president for student affairs — is to provide leadership and direction to these services and programs. The position has evolved in the past three decades and at most colleges and universities is now part of the management team, which includes the president and the principal officers for development and for academic, financial, and student affairs. Chief student affairs officers have emerged as leaders who can contribute substantially to the quality of campus life. The position is gaining strength and visibility as the responsibilities associated with it increase; now is an appropriate time to examine and assess it. This book focuses on the leadership role of chief student affairs officers. CSAOs are highly visible leaders on campus and in their communities and must respond effectively to the often conflicting expectations of diverse constituencies: students, parents, presidents, faculty, administrative colleagues, the community, alumni, legislators, and their own staff. As leaders, they are expected to be good managers, delivering timely services to students while handling large budgets efficiently; effective mediators, resolving difficult disputes and campus conflicts; and sound educators, planning and putting into effect successful cocurricular programs for students.

Purpose and Intended Audience

The position of chief student affairs officer is challenging and stressful, and it is one of critical importance to colleges and universities. Because it is still a relatively new position, though, and because colleges and universities are increasingly departmentalized, the CSAO's role is not very well understood by others in higher education. The primary purpose of this book is to contribute to understanding of what chief student affairs officers do, so that they can carry out the responsibilities of the position more effectively. One intended audience, therefore, is presidents, chief academic, financial, and development officers, governing board members, and faculty. The quality of the education and services available to students will certainly improve if there is more cooperation among the major administrative and academic components of institutions, and such cooperation is likelier if there is better understanding of the chief student affairs officer's function. I also hope that reading *The Chief Student Affairs Officer* will assist presidents and search committee members as they consider the qualifications and backgrounds of individuals seeking the position.

The book is directed as well to practicing chief student affairs officers, to those who aspire to the position, and to faculty teaching in graduate programs designed to prepare people for administrative leadership positions in higher education. Finally, the book is intended to upgrade the level of performance of chief student affairs officers themselves and to assist colleges and universities in clarifying the kind of leadership they can reasonably expect from administrators holding the position.

Overview of the Contents

Part One of *The Chief Student Affairs Officer* consists of four chapters that survey the CSAO's responsibilities as a campus leader. The first chapter serves as an introduction to the position, describing the various roles and functions associated with it and discussing its origins and evolution. The chief student affairs officer's special relationships with the president and other major administrative officers of the institution are the focus of Chapter Two. Particular consideration is given to the student affairs leader's role on the management team. Chapter Three describes the crucial and complex relationship between the chief student affairs officer and the students. The chapter discusses the diversity of student communities and the implications of their varying expectations for the student affairs leader. The chief student affairs officer's major constituencies are described in Chapter Four. One of the primary challenges of the office is to balance the sometimes contradictory needs and wishes of faculty, administrative colleagues, presidents, students, and community members.

The three chapters that Part Two comprises focus on the primary administrative functions of the chief student affairs officer: management, mediation, and education. Chapter Five, which concerns the student affairs leader as manager, describes organizational, financial, and supervisory responsibilities. Chapter Six, which discusses the chief student affairs officer as mediator, proposes specific strategies for effective mediation of campus problems. Chapter Seven presents the chief student affairs officer as educator, the most important function of the position. Each of these roles is critical to the success of the chief student affairs officer, and failure to do well in any of them will result in unacceptable performance. Case examples of management, mediation, and educational problems are presented, along with suggestions for good practice in each area.

The two chapters that make up Part Three explore professional concerns and commitments. Chapter Eight focuses on the need to assess the professional effectiveness of chief student affairs officers and describes the complexities of determining adequate evaluative criteria. In Chapter Nine I speculate about trends likely to affect the future development of the position, and I offer modest suggestions to institutions, current practitioners, and those who aspire to the position.

Acknowledgments

I am indebted to all the people who have contributed in so many ways to this book. The student affairs staffs at the University of Florida, Iowa State University, and Michigan State University all taught me more than I could ever convey in writing, and their support and friendship over the past thirty years are gratefully acknowledged. I also want to express my appreciation for the numerous insights I have gained over the years from two colleagues at the University of Florida: Robert A. Bryan, provost, and the late William Elmore, vice president for administrative affairs. I have been very fortunate to work with many outstanding presidents, and the support and understanding of Robert Parks, E. T. York, Robert Q. Marston, Marshall M. Criser, and John V. Lombardi are gratefully acknowledged, as well.

I have benefited greatly over the years from a close relationship with the National Association of Student Personnel Administrators, and from the many members of that organization who have shared their knowledge and wisdom with me. I am particularly indebted to Robert Etheridge at Miami University, my long-time mentor and friend; also Donald Adams at Drake University; Margaret Barr at Texas Christian University; Larry Ebbers at Iowa State University; Thomas Goodale at Virginia Technological University; George Kuh at Indiana University; James Lyons at Stanford University; and James Rhatigan at Wichita State University. I also want to acknowledge and thank my close colleagues in the Vice Presidents Group, who have given me more ideas and useful advice than I can ever return.

My friendships with Thomas Barnum, William Inskeep, and James Twitchell have provided me with insights about higher education that could not have been gained in any other way. I appreciate their candor and advice.

I am indebted to Sarah Resnick Carswell, Carolyn Drummond, and Priscilla Williams in the student affairs office at the University of Florida for their assistance in preparing the manuscript. They made helpful suggestions about the format as well.

To the thousands of students I have known and worked with over the past thirty years in student affairs, I express my thanks for their friendship. The education of students is the principal aim of chief student affairs officers.

It has been a special pleasure and privilege to work with Ursula Delworth, professor of education at the University of Iowa, whose editorial skills and gentle suggestions resulted in a greatly strengthened manuscript. The high quality of many publications in the student affairs literature is attributable to her effective editorial leadership.

I thank Sue Sandeen for providing me with the most valuable insight regarding higher education and its problems, as well as the most honest criticism of my work. Finally, *The Chief Student Affairs Officer* is dedicated to two highly promising educators, Sara Sandeen Kennedy and Anne Sandeen Schatz, who are already discovering the joys and possibilities of the world of education.

Gainesville, Florida   Arthur Sandeen
June 1991

THE AUTHOR

Arthur Sandeen is vice president for student affairs and professor of educational leadership at the University of Florida. He
received his B.A. degree (1960) from Miami University (Ohio)
in psychology and religion, his M.A. degree (1962) from Michigan State University in college personnel administration, and
his Ph.D. degree (1965) from Michigan State University in administration and higher education. He also received a diploma
from the Institute for Educational Management at Harvard
University in 1984.

Sandeen has served as associate director of residence hall
programs at Michigan State University (1965–1967), as associate
dean of students at Iowa State University (1967–68), as dean
of students at Iowa State University (1968–1973), and as vice
president for student affairs at the University of Florida since
1973. He was president of the National Association of Student
Personnel Administrators in 1977–78 and is the recipient of the
Fred Turner Award for Outstanding Service (1983) and the Scott
Goodnight Award for Outstanding Performance as a Dean
(1990). He also served as chairman of the committee that wrote
the National Association of Student Personnel Administrators'
1987 publication *A Perspective on Student Affairs,* commemorating
the fiftieth anniversary of *The Student Personnel Point of View.*

Sandeen is the author of *Undergraduate Education: Conflict
and Change* (1976) and of numerous articles and chapters in student affairs publications. He has also served as a consultant to
several colleges and universities on student affairs policies, practices, and organization.

Part One

The Chief Student Affairs Officer as Campus Leader

1

The Evolving Complexity
of Student Affairs
Leadership

"Why would that college permit its students to behave that
way?"
"I'm disgusted with the large number of college students
getting all those loans and then not paying them back."
"You know they're not teaching those young kids any
values these days in college."
"It's outrageous; it's going to cost me $18,000 to send my
daughter to college for just one year!"
"My husband and I are alums of that school, and they
won't even consider admitting our son."
"I'm very worried about how safe it is in our daughter's
dorm room; I think the college should provide better
security."
"Now I'm really mad; all that money I paid to that college, and they can't even find my son a good job!"

The concerns reflected in these statements have a great
deal to do with why student affairs exists in American higher
education. Colleges and universities are expected to provide personal support and extensive services to students, and all of these
efforts need to be coordinated and managed by someone. In the
past thirty years, the position of chief student affairs officer
(CSAO) has emerged to address this need.

The CSAO is part of the institutional management and leadership team; he or she manages and directs the various services, programs, and policies for students that support the educational and social objectives of colleges and universities. The two most common titles for the CSAO position are now vice president for student affairs and dean of student affairs. The position has evolved over a period of 100 years from a collegiate, almost parental concern for student welfare to the current complex array of services and programs for students that extend throughout the campus. This chapter describes the current roles, functions, and relationships of the position, and presents special problems, strategies, and suggestions.

Key Roles

The CSAO in American higher education today has a broad range of responsibilities — admissions, registration, and financial aid; student physical and mental health; housing, activities, and student unions; career services and placement; recreation and intercollegiate athletics; student judicial affairs and campus security; child care; and various academic support services. At some colleges and universities, the CSAO also has responsibility for the campus bus system, the major multipurpose campus facility, programs for disabled students, and the institutional assessment program. Within each of these major functions, of course, there may be additional important responsibilities. For example, within the activities area, there may be a student leadership development program, minority student cultural centers, religious advising, a women's educational center, and a student volunteer office. In the admissions office, there may be a recruitment and retention center, an office of high school and community college relations, and an office for new-student orientation. Special academic support programs may include academic advising, tutoring and remedial services, and speech and hearing clinics. On a large campus, there may be more than 1,000 full-time staff in the student affairs division; on a campus of 1,500 students, fewer than 20 student affairs personnel.

The CSAO is expected to define and organize these services and programs for the institution, and ensure that they are managed and delivered effectively. The scope and functions of the division are developed by the student affairs leader, along with the president and governing board, in accordance with the distinctive purpose of the institution. The CSAO is the principal advocate for student needs at the institution, and thus often competes with academic, financial, and development administrators for available resources.

The CSAO is expected to assume several roles. The most important are manager, mediator, and educator. With many services and programs as part of the division of student affairs, effective personnel and fiscal management is essential. Establishing clear objectives that are known, understood, and accepted by the campus community is part of this management task as well. The fiscal responsibility often exceeds several million dollars, and it is the duty of the CSAO to manage these financial resources effectively. With large numbers of professional, support, and student staff in the student affairs division, the CSAO must establish personnel practices that enable them to perform their duties, participate in the decision-making process, and have opportunities for professional advancement and growth. Perhaps the most important management responsibility is to ensure that the various services and programs are operating at a high level of quality in accordance with their objectives. In most cases, of course, this means that the services and programs must be well received and frequently used by students. The CSAO must also have in place some regular means of assessment to indicate how students and others are reacting to these services and programs.

The CSAO often assumes a mediating role with various groups, both on and off the campus. At both large and small institutions, there are many student groups that compete for resources, access, and student power. CSAOs may intervene and help solve student organizational disputes. More frequently, the CSAO is a mediator — between students and the president; between the institution and students' parents; between the faculty senate and the students; between the community and the students; and between student affairs staff and the faculty. There are often conflicting expectations and perceptions among these groups, and the effectiveness of CSAOs is frequently viewed as a function of how successful they are in negotiating problems. This "buffer" or "peacemaker" role usually extends to the handling of various campus crises, especially those associated with some form of student demonstration or protest. The CSAO is expected to play the major leadership role in the institution's effort to settle student-related crises.

Most student affairs leaders define their primary responsibility as educators. Programs, services, and policies are developed in the student affairs division that support the institution's distinct educational mission and the behavioral and social goals it has for its students. The CSAO's major responsibility is to see that everything that occurs within the student affairs division is in support of these goals. This necessarily places the CSAO in regular contact with the principal academic officer of the university, its deans, and the faculty. It compels the CSAO to have a well-defined educational philosophy that is compatible with the institution, credible with faculty and students, and endorsed by the president and the governing board. It also requires that the CSAO be able to articulate the educational and cocurricular programs to people outside the institution in a way that gains their understanding and support.

It is possible, of course, for CSAOs to face ethical dilemmas in their work: The deeds of institutions may not always match their personal beliefs, or certain priorities may conflict with what CSAOs think is in the best interests of students. It is essential that student affairs leaders understand and accept the educational goals and purposes of their institutions at the time they are appointed, and that they be candid with the president and others about their own priorities. A poor fit between the university and the CSAO serves neither well. The chief student affairs administrator serves at the pleasure of the president, and so it is critical that their goals, priorities, and styles be compatible. It is best to confront differences at the time of appointment, but if CSAOs face ethical or other dilemmas even after such efforts, it is their responsibility to be straightforward with the president and to take action consistent with their professional commitments. Open and diplomatic relations with various constituent groups both on and off campus are essential to the success of the CSAO as well. Most student affairs leaders recognize that their effectiveness depends not only on the support of their president but also on their acceptance by these groups; they understand, too, that when such support and acceptance are eroded or compromised, their institutions will probably replace them.

The student affairs profession is young and is still evolving. There is significant variation from one campus to another regarding the responsibilities and administrative portfolios of CSAOs. While this variation may reflect institutional traditions and academic emphases, it may also reflect the quality of leadership provided by the CSAO. If the student affairs program has as its sole focus such matters as student conduct and psychological counseling, then it will remain on the educational sidelines of higher education, and is not likely to be viewed by faculty, students, and others as vital to the institution's future. However, on many campuses of the 1990s, the student affairs component of the institution plays a critical role in shaping the composition of the student body, managing the various services and programs designed to assist students, and contributing to the quality and content of the teaching program. This expanded role is most often the result of the energetic and persuasive efforts of a CSAO. Few presidents, chief academic officers, or faculty senates have clearly in mind what they should expect from a CSAO; it is largely up to the person holding this position to inform and convince others in the institution what needs to be accomplished, and how. Job descriptions are not very meaningful for CSAOs; their jobs really consist of developing resources, negotiating with groups, and convincing others of the need for programs and services.

The position of CSAO is currently enjoying its greatest visibility and influence since the establishment of the student affairs profession in about 1890. It has grown into its current status because of the increasingly complex needs of institutions, and because of the ability of many CSAOs to articulate institutional problems clearly and to deliver effective programs address-

ing them. However, there is still much work to be done in helping significant numbers of colleges and universities give greater
prominence to their student affairs programs. By presenting a
realistic view of the exciting activities being conducted by student affairs leaders now on many campuses, this book may contribute to that movement.

Why Examine the Role of the CSAO?

American higher education has been subjected to a great deal
of public scrutiny in the past twenty years, as colleges and universities have assumed such a critical role in the nation's future.
They are expected to pass on the intellectual heritage and at
the same time encourage critical thinking; transmit cultural
values while also stimulating consideration of new norms; prepare students for a technological society while also making them
humane and caring citizens; and provide objective and rational
forums for the discussion of critical issues while also helping society solve its social problems. Alan Bloom's book *The Closing
of the American Mind* (1987) was on the nation's best-seller list
for almost a year — evidence that the public is very concerned
about what happens in its colleges and universities. The several
national reports (National Institute of Education, 1985; Bennett, 1985; National Governors' Association, 1986; Boyer, 1987;
American Association of State Colleges and Universities, 1986;
Education Commission of the States, 1986) on reform in higher
education, each with a special admonition to institutions to address the needs of students more effectively, further attest to the
current period of national debate. Most recently, Bruce Wilshire's book *The Moral Collapse of the University* (1989) adds another
provocative voice to this important discussion.

The issues raised in this current debate about higher education relate directly to the major concerns of the CSAO: access to college, student diversity, student and institutional costs,
quality of life, and the assessment of student and educational
outcomes. It is perhaps fortuitous that this highly visible and
serious debate about higher education's purposes should coin-
cide with the time that many CSAOs have emerged as vital parts

of their institutions. The opportunities for positive change have never been more attractive.

It is also an appropriate time to examine the CSAO position because it has changed in significant ways over the last generation. Student affairs has often been viewed by others within the college or university as a peripheral or adjunct service, but in the past twenty-five years, many CSAOs have helped to move student affairs into the main educational arena of the campus. The position is now part of the central management team of the institution and has assumed responsibilities it did not include years ago, and this "news" ought to be made known to others in and out of higher education. Faculty, academic deans, business officers, governing boards, and (where appropriate) state higher education officials and legislators need to be made aware of the changes. They may hold stereotypic notions of what a CSAO's role is, and a current discussion of actual responsibilities may serve to correct some old perceptions.

The administration of student affairs programs in higher education is in an important transition period. CSAOs are facing new challenges and have new opportunities to participate in the management of their institutions. The major issues and problems facing colleges and universities now are so critical, and the public's stake in these matters is so important, that they have to be addressed; if the leadership and initiative are not forthcoming from CSAOs, the gap will be filled in some other way, perhaps even from outside the institution. For some, these challenges will seem too daunting, and they will choose to stay in the comfortable corners of the campus where they have been working for years; others will seize the current opportunities with energy and high expectations. Thus, it is a critical time for CSAOs themselves, and the leadership and initiative they are able to assume in this decade are likely to have a major impact on the nature and quality of student affairs in future years.

The expectations others have for the CSAO represent another reason why it is useful to examine this position now. Students, and especially their parents, are likely to view the institution as consumers, and expect timely, affordable, and high-quality services in areas where institutions have not been active before. Presidents and college financial administrators expect the CSAO to be knowledgeable about money, computers, and fund raising. Academic deans expect CSAOs to assist in meeting their educational and service goals for students. Governing board members and legislative leaders may expect the CSAO to respond to their special needs. The student affairs staff itself has become more sophisticated professionally in the past several years, and may have expectations for the CSAO that conflict with those of others in the institution. All of these expectations for the CSAO clearly suggest that the position is at a critical stage in its young life, and that an examination of its roles and functions is timely.

A Brief History

Several useful historical accounts about the development of the student affairs profession exist (for example, Leonard, 1956; Knock, 1985; Fenske, 1989), so there is no need to duplicate those in this space. However, none of these authors has specifically addressed the evolution of the CSAO's position, which has occurred only recently. An understanding of these origins may contribute to a better understanding of the current roles and functions of the position.

When Charles Eliot assumed the presidency of Harvard in 1869, it was clear that his new elective system would bring significant changes to all aspects of the institution. One of his first acts as president was to appoint Ephraim Gurney, a professor of history, as dean of the college. Dean Gurney's assignment included responsibilities for instruction, registration, and student welfare. This delegation of duties enabled President Eliot to concentrate his own efforts on transforming Harvard from a college to a university. During the 1890–91 academic year, Eliot decided to divide the deanship, since Harvard's enrollment had grown and it was now the largest college in the country. Charles Dunbar became dean of the faculty, and shy thirty-five-year-old English instructor, LeBaron Russell Briggs, became dean of the college.

President Eliot's action was greeted with surprise and skepticism by most of the faculty. What, after all, was the new dean to do? It seemed that young Dean Briggs was not entirely clear himself! But President Eliot had discovered that the students were visiting with Professor Briggs on every type of problem, and the appointment seemed a logical formalization of this fine relationship. Moreover, as Eliot later admitted, having Briggs in the position of dean relieved the president of some very unpleasant problems (Cowley, 1949). It also enabled the faculty to get on with the all-important business of creating a university, and reinforced the separation of student life from classroom work.

Although he carried the title of dean of the college, Dean Briggs was actually the first dean of men, since all the students at Harvard were male. He was the embodiment of the compassionate, loving, patient father figure. He took flowers to the sick, visited students in the hospital, and wrote to parents about their sons (Fley, 1977). His kindly, uncanny ability to assist students became legendary, and his biography (Brown, 1926) and writings (Briggs, 1900) are still sources of inspiration to student affairs staff today.

When Oberlin College opened its doors in 1833, it made a courageous decision to admit women to its student body. The "female department" was later headed by Mrs. Adelia Johnston, who came to Oberlin in 1870. By the time she left the college in 1900, she had become Dean Johnston. At about the same time, the University of Michigan established a special "health program" for its women students, and Eliza Mosher, M.D., was appointed dean of women in 1892 (Holmes, 1939). But it was an outstanding Boston educator, Marion Talbot, recruited by President William Rainey Harper to join the exciting new University of Chicago, who was to become the pioneering dean of women (Fley, 1978). Her duties on behalf of the women students at Chicago paralleled those of Dean Briggs at Harvard for the men. Besides providing for the daily needs, welfare, and health of the students, Dean Talbot worked to define new roles for women, and argued for a curriculum that would prepare them for productive lives. Dean Talbot called the first national meeting for deans of women in 1903, and together with her colleague, Lois Kimball Mathews of the University of Wisconsin, helped to advance the position throughout higher education. In a remarkable book, Mathews (1915) argued that the main role of the dean of women was not that of a disciplinarian or chaperon but an expert on women's education in a coeducational institution.

Institutions everywhere followed the lead of Harvard and Chicago, and deans of men and deans of women were appointed at most colleges and universities by 1910. There was wide variation in their duties, but all assumed the role of social welfare workers for their students. Colleges were growing and becoming more complex. It was perhaps inevitable that the increasing departmentalization of institutions would result in a separation of student life from the more formal classroom work of the campus. As Frederick Rudolph (1965) suggested, to resist many of the dehumanizing consequences of organization was, of course, a losing proposition, but the early deans were an institutional expression of an unofficial longing to do so. The deans represented an effort to maintain collegiate and humane values in an atmosphere of increasing scholarship and specialization.

College and university enrollments continued to increase and the administrative organizations of institutions eventually came to include specific offices for health services, counseling, activities, admissions, vocational guidance, and registration. By the 1930s, there was growing concern that this proliferation of services needed coordination and direction. On most campuses, some of the services reported to the president, some to the business officer, and others to the registrar or the academic dean. This often resulted in confusion for the student and an expensive duplication of services for the college.

In a landmark address entitled "The Disappearing Dean of Men" (1937), W. H. Cowley accurately predicted what was happening in student affairs. A new institutional officer was now being appointed at colleges and universities to coordinate and direct all the institutional services related to the out-of-class experiences of students. The title of this new administrator was usually dean of students or dean of student affairs. Victor I. Moore at the University of Texas and I. D. Putnam of the

University of California, Berkeley, were among the first to be granted the title of dean of student affairs in the 1930s. By the 1950s, Cowley's prediction had become a reality, and most colleges and universities had established one campuswide dean for student-related functions. The titles of dean of men and dean of women had almost disappeared by 1960, as campus life was no longer as segregated by gender as it had been. Student affairs organizations became unified, headed by one administrator.

Not surprisingly, there was resistance to this increasing specialization and administrative growth. Faculty on some campuses were concerned that these new appointments would place a drain on what they considered more important academic resources; others did not want to see any additional power structures established within the academy. There was resistance within the student affairs community as well: Some viewed the new consolidated organization as a threat to the autonomy they had previously enjoyed. Deans of men and women had often established their own separate "fiefdoms" on campus, and they were not very enthusiastic about relinquishing their authority to a new administrative structure. But there was also the kind of resistance described by Jacques Barzun in an article entitled "Deans Within Deans" (1945, p. 81): "There has grown up a class of professional administrators, not members of the faculty, but academic middlemen, who find university life congenial and the students interesting, but who would just as readily manage a brewery or a bank for all the attachment they feel towards learning."

Thus, while almost all colleges and universities were establishing a centralized administrative structure for student affairs, this change often took place in an atmosphere of adversity and resentment. The early deans of men and women struggled for almost fifty years to establish their roles on campuses; now, the newly appointed deans of student affairs were to face a similar uphill battle for acceptance in the academic community.

The huge increases in enrollment, the social upheavals in society and on the campuses, and the greatly increased emphasis on research and scholarship of the 1960s made it possible and perhaps even necessary for the new centralized student affairs administration to survive. Most faculty were so engrossed in their own specialized activities that they seldom concerned themselves with what was happening in the student affairs organization. More important, what the student affairs staff was now doing became critical to the institution for the first time. The civil rights movement and the Vietnam War forced institutions to deal with issues of gender and racial equity, treatment of students as citizens with constitutional rights, and student participation in campus governance. This highly volatile situation catapulted student affairs leaders into highly visible roles on their campuses, and resulted in the widespread establishment of the position of vice president for student affairs. By 1972, 18 percent of chief student affairs administrators had been granted the title of vice president (Crookston, 1974), and in 1989, vice president was the most commonly used title for the CSAO in higher education (National Association of Student Personnel Administrators, 1989).

To reiterate, the CSAO has evolved over a period of 100 years from the early dean of men and dean of women, to the deans of student affairs, and now to the vice president for student affairs. Responsibilities have multiplied during this period, and it is now one of the major administrative leadership components of most colleges and universities, charged with coordinating and directing the various campus programs and service for students.

Qualities and Professional Skills

The early deans, of course, were recruited from the ranks of the faculty. Presidents usually selected faculty who had demonstrated a special interest in students and who were respected and popular teachers. Few had had any administrative experience, and there was wide variation in the way they conducted their offices. It was not long before efforts were underway to develop formal graduate programs designed to prepare those who aspired to become deans. The first master's degree, "Diploma for Dean of Women," was granted at the Teachers College at Columbia University in 1914 (Lloyd-Jones, 1949). Graduate programs were developed at Minnesota, Syracuse,

Northwestern, and many other institutions, as the young profession sought ways to upgrade the skills and knowledge of its members and to legitimize its standing in the academic community. Despite the growth of these graduate programs, their major impact for many years was limited to improving the preparation of those selected to be counselors, admissions officers, housing staff, and student activities directors. Most of the CSAOs continued to be selected from the ranks of the faculty, or another administrative area, a trend that continued until as late as 1970 (Brooks and Avila, 1974). This was probably a function of the president's desire to secure support and credibility for student affairs on the campus from the faculty. On some campuses, it also reflected long-standing perceptions that those who worked in student affairs were primarily oriented toward counseling and were not well suited for a major administrative role.

As the student affairs field became increasingly professionalized, chief student affairs administrators who had received the benefits of formal preparation for their positions became more visible and successful. Many demonstrated to their institutions that they were capable of managing and directing a large administrative organization and that they could contribute positively to the quality of life on the campus as well. This success, more than any other factor, has led to the current position of considerable influence now enjoyed by CSAOs on scores of campuses. It has also resulted in higher expectations by presidents, governing board members, faculty, other administrators, and students. And it has meant the addition of responsibilities not formerly part of student affairs.

Most CSAOs have now earned the doctoral degree, and most advertisements for vice presidents for student affairs positions now specify this degree as a minimum qualification (Lunsford, 1984). Various studies (for example, Kuh, Evans, and Duke, 1983; Ostroth, Efird, and Lerman, 1984; Rickard, 1985) of CSAOs conducted in recent years indicate that most have the doctorate, that a majority are white males, that approximately 12 percent are women, and that about 9 percent are minorities. The majority of female CSAOs are found in private institutions, and minority CSAOs are more frequently found in large public universities.

CSAOs understand that different groups have varying expectations of them. They believe they must be a wizard with the students, a dove with the faculty, a Professor Chips with alumni, and a dragon for the president. These widely diverse roles require the special qualifications and competencies found in chief student affairs officers today.

While few possess all the myriad skills necessary to meet the varying demands of the CSAO position, there are broad areas of competence that are needed by all. Because of the heavy administrative and fiscal responsibilities, extensive skills in management and decision making are essential. At the University of California, Davis, for example, the vice chancellor for student affairs administers a budget in excess of $30 million and a staff of more than 500. With student, administrative, and community groups competing for space, resources, and power, CSAOs must also have well-developed mediation skills. This is true even at smaller institutions, where CSAOs may find themselves acting as the chief negotiators in settling conflicts among student groups, community organizations, and faculty. They are also expected to contribute to the overall educational program on the campus and to improve the quality of student life. This requires them to have the appropriate academic credentials to be accepted by the faculty, and, equally important, the ability to articulate credible ideas and programs that can become operationally effective for students. For example, the vice chancellor for student affairs at Texas Christian University has developed a two-year student leadership program consisting of several classes. She has also been successful in securing financial support for the program.

Because CSAOs are often the most visible administrators on the campus other than the president, they are subjected to a great deal of public scrutiny by students, faculty, other administrators, alumni, and the press. Such regular exposure to criticism requires patience, self-confidence, and a sense of humor. The volatile nature of the issues faced, and the lack of concrete ways of evaluating the success of the student affairs leader, make the position particularly vulnerable to attack. The CSAO's position is not a comfortable one; it is filled with turmoil and stress, and thus requires a person who is able and willing to deal with those strains. The most successful CSAOs are those who seem to thrive on this emotional ambiguity by viewing it as an exciting educational challenge; the inability of others to handle this challenge is the major reason they are removed from their position, or seek another, quieter professional activity on their own.

Because the responsibilities of the position have become more extensive in the past twenty-five years, the knowledge and skills required by the CSAOs have increased. In addition to formal graduate preparation in student affairs administration, the CSAO needs skills in financial management, the administration of computer services, fund raising, legal and security matters, and multicultural education. While such needs are well known to practicing CSAOs, graduate programs in higher education and student personnel administration have been slow to adapt their curricula to match current realities. This has resulted in a proliferation of special institutes for the continuing education of CSAOs. It has also led to a tendency for presidents to select CSAOs with backgrounds in academic and fiscal management in addition to their expertise in student affairs administration.

Certain skills may be more important than others at different institutions. At a residential liberal arts college of 1,500 students, effective personal mediation may be more important than fiscal management. At a new, urban, commuter university, the ability to identify needs, secure resources, and organize and deliver effective programs may be more important than mediation. At a highly selective, large independent university, where many groups are vying for access and where there are frequent clashes among different cultures, the CSAO will need to be especially able in educational and mediation skills. At a nonselective, medium-size college in a state with a declining high school age population, the CSAO will be expected to have exceptional management skills, especially in building and maintaining enrollment.

Management, mediation, and educational skills are essential to all CSAOs, but there must be a good fit between the particular skills and abilities of the major student affairs leader and the institution. Moreover, what a particular college or university needs in a CSAO may change over a period of time, depending on its problems and priorities. Some chief student affairs administrators who were very effective in helping their institutions deal with the student unrest of the 1960s and early 1970s have found they are ill equipped to address the fiscal management and consumer services needs of the 1990s, and have left their positions. Other CSAOs may have as their top priority creating new educational opportunities for students when the most pressing need of the institution is for additional enrollment. The needs of colleges and universities change; the skills and abilities of the chief student affairs administrators hired to serve them must also change to meet these needs.

2

Supporting
and Assisting
the President

College presidents might have been able to function as academic monarchs in the past, but today they have much more complex roles as leaders. Today's institutions of higher education are closely interrelated with the rest of society, and they are also expected to solve many of its most pressing social and economic problems. These problems do not lend themselves to narrowly defined solutions; they require the participation and expertise of people from many areas — including student affairs.

Student affairs has become a distinct part of the organizational structure of colleges and universities. CSAOs have specific assignments for student matters, but in addition they operate as part of the institution's team, along with the president and the other vice presidents. All the senior officers share in the responsibility for the policies and programs of the institution. This active participation in the academic, financial, legislative, and development aspects of the institution is relatively new for CSAOs, and is an important challenge for the 1990s.

The dramatic changes that have occurred in corporate management in the past two decades have also had an impact on how colleges and universities conduct their business. However, while many of the managerial and administrative issues faced by universities are similar to those in the corporate world, there are important differences (Millett, 1962). The faculty is a highly diverse, intellectually sophisticated group of professionals whose primary commitment is likely to be to their academic discipline, not necessarily to their institution. Moreover, as professionals, they do not often view themselves as employees in a line relationship to any administrator, and they generally govern their own activities. The students are both the "customers" and the "product," but often expect to be active participants in deciding the process and the content of their own education. In successful educational programs, students are not simply passive consumers, but are, in effect, junior colleagues with the faculty. The alumni, the community, the state government, the governing board, corporations, and donors may all feel they have some stake in the management and administration of the institution. This complex structure is captured in the concept of "multiversity" that Clark Kerr (1982) presented in his famous lectures at Harvard.

Because of the incredible complexity of modern colleges and universities and the multiple constituencies they face, the management styles of leaders in higher education have changed. These institutions are no longer managed by "hero-bureaucrats" (Baldridge and Deal, 1983), but by leaders who should be characterized as mediators and academic statesmen. Robert Dahl's (1961, p. 204) description of the political role of a big-city mayor also applies to the current college president: "The mayor was not at the peak of a pyramid, but rather at the center of interacting circles. He rarely pressed, appealed, reasoned, promised, initiated, demanded, even threatened, but he most needed support and acquiescence from other leaders who simply could not be commanded. Because he could not command, he had to bargain."

Perhaps the most dramatic change has been the emphasis on developing an effective management team, consisting of the president and the chief administrative officers of the college responsible for academic programs, financial affairs, development, and student affairs. The shift toward participatory management and collaboration has been the subject of several books in higher education and management (Argyris, 1982; Keller, 1983; Powers and Powers, 1983; Varney, 1989), and a dominant theme at national conferences and professional development institutes. In a recent study examining twenty highly successful colleges and universities, Gilley, Fulmer, and Reithlingsbroefer (1986, p. 29) found that an emphasis on teamwork and the creation of strong administrative teams were critical reasons for achievement in all cases. In another study, Kouzes and Posner (1987, p. 193) found that nothing extraordinary was accomplished in any college without the active effort and support of many people. In their landmark work, Peters and Waterman (1982) identified a strong emphasis on the development of collaboration and teamwork in the nation's best-run companies.

All effective management teams stress interaction and cooperation. It is not always easy to accomplish this in a college or university, since the various vice presidents are often competing with each other for institutional resources. It is also very likely that there will be differing views about academic priorities, building plans, space allocation, fund-raising strategies, student costs, admissions standards, and many other issues. In the absence of a team approach, the vice presidents may establish their own separate units, purposely insulated from each other to protect and defend "their" resources and policies. When this happens, the administration of the college becomes disjointed, resources are poorly used, and turmoil, confusion, and frustration usually result. However, if the president and the vice presidents can view major problems as institutionwide issues involving a shared mission, then they may become a real team. The essence of the management team concept is to collaborate and to share, not to compete and to protect.

The emergence of the management team in higher education is of great importance to the CSAO. It means that the position has a new level of institutional influence and that student affairs agendas are considered an integral part of institutional policies and priorities on a regular basis. It also means that CSAOs are now expected to contribute to the overall success of the institution. Finally, it means that CSAOs must understand and be able to work effectively with all the team members: the president, the chief academic officer, the chief financial officer, and the chief development officer.

Relationship to the President

It is the president who makes it possible for CSAOs to do their jobs. The president appoints the major student affairs leader, decides what resources are made available, approves and defends major policies and programs, and evaluates performance on a regular basis. If presidents are unsupportive, inconsistent, or unpredictable, the student affairs leader will achieve very little success. If presidents do not clearly understand the complex nature of the CSAO's responsibilities, little will be accomplished. The president is clearly the most critical person in any success a CSAO can have at the institution. If the president's support and understanding are not present, the CSAO should most likely seek employment at another institution.

The more time and effort CSAOs give to informing their president about student-related problems, the more likely they will be to win the support and confidence of the president. The most effective CSAOs do not want their presidents looking over their shoulders, becoming involved in the day-to-day administration of the student affairs division. They do want and need presidents who understand them, what they are working to accomplish, and what they need to be successful. It is the responsibility of CSAOs to earn the support of their presidents through their actions.

While institutions have many similarities, there are distinct differences, and the priorities and styles of one president may vary significantly from those of another. And even within the same institution, when a president resigns or retires, his or her successor may introduce a new set of expectations. Indeed, Clark Kerr (1984, p. xviii) reports that 30 percent of presidents turn over every two years, with the average tenure in office being about seven years.

The most important concern for a person seeking a CSAO position is a good fit with the institution's president. This requires a candid sharing of educational philosophies, administrative styles, and personal backgrounds. Because the issues faced are frequently volatile, the president and the CSAO must have no doubts about each other's priorities and beliefs. They must be able to make mutual decisions on the basis of trust. If this is not possible, the results may be damaging to students and embarrassing for the institution. The president must have absolute faith in the CSAO's judgment, and this can only be developed if they work together closely as part of a management team.

It is essential for the CSAO to understand the role of the president. He or she should recognize that the president's priorities must often be with the governing board, and that the increasing fractionalization of the campus into special interest groups has made the position very stressful. As Kerr and Gade (1986, p. xiv) note, "Presidents work in environments of mixed constituencies, of conflicts of interests, of constant time pressures, of evaluations by many persons on the basis of many contrasting tests of performance, of uncertainties about their endurance in the position." The constituencies the president faces shift in membership and size, and as Walker (1979, p. 71) suggests, "The president is vulnerable and recognizes the hazard that the support he or she currently enjoys may be withdrawn at any time." To get the president's attention and commitment, the CSAO will have to be clear and persuasive about the objectives of the student affairs program. A major cause for the lack of success of CSAOs has been their inability to define the student affairs program to their presidents in understandable and credible terms. Few presidents have the time or the patience for lengthy psychosocial explanations of every campus problem or issue; they need succinct, comprehensible explanations and concrete proposals for solutions.

The CSAO is the primary institutional advocate for students and, as a result, is likely to argue for resources and policy decisions that are sometimes not popular with the president. As James Fisher (1984, p. 17), an experienced president, put it, "Company types do not work well in the CSAO position." The CSAO must be willing to argue with the president in representing the needs of the students, but must also remain steadfastly loyal to whatever decision is eventually made. The CSAO serves at the pleasure of the president, and must recognize that all policies and programs within the student affairs division must have the president's support.

It is the responsibility of the student affairs leader to inform and educate the president about the student body, and the various services and programs necessary to meet their needs. Few presidents have professional backgrounds in student affairs, and they may have little information about what to expect from the CSAO. It is not uncommon for new presidents to assume that the primary function of student affairs is to keep the campus quiet and civil, or to see little or no relationship between the teaching program and student affairs. The CSAO must help the president learn about student affairs, and the various functions, policies, and programs in the division. This cannot be done overnight. It will usually take at least a year of conversation, involvement in day-to-day issues and problems, and a carefully planned exposure to a variety of student-related activities.

The CSAO should be the campus expert on how students and other groups respond to the president, and should arrange public contacts accordingly. While the student affairs leader cannot, of course, orchestrate all student and media contacts for the president, it is important to make sure that the president is not surprised or unprepared for any issue. One of the key responsibilities of CSAOs, especially when the president is newly appointed, is to ensure that the president is not put in an embarrassing position with students or others in any public forum, particularly in early appearances on campus. If the president is invited to speak at a large residence hall and does not know in advance that reporters from the local television station will be there to record any responses to irate student complaints about long registration lines, it will be embarrassing for the president and disastrous for the CSAO! Early in the president's tenure, it is wise for the CSAO to arrange public appearances that virtually guarantee success and positive feedback from students. But no president can escape the lively challenges that students delight in presenting to them, especially in public. CSAOs must make sure their presidents are well informed about campus issues and problems and know how to respond to them. Some presidents genuinely enjoy the combative give-and-take in public forums with students, and as a result are viewed as open, concerned, and humane academic leaders. Others are not at all inclined to participate in such forums, and should be advised to avoid them.

With the tremendous diversity of students on most campuses, the CSAO must be sure the president does not show preference for one group of students over another. Presidents may feel most comfortable with students in the marching band or on the gymnastics team, but if they never visit a sorority house or a campus religious organization, it is very likely to be noticed and eventually resented by these groups. It is very important for the CSAO to arrange regular contacts for the president with minority student organizations, disabled students, and international students. Without such contacts, the president's public pronouncements about the institution's desire to improve access to special groups may seem hollow.

Most presidents will need good advice and preparation to be effective with student groups, which vary widely in their political, religious, social, and ethnic orientations. In one week, the president may speak at a banquet of the Chinese Student Organization, meet to hear the concerns of the Black Law Student Association, be asked by the campus chapter of the National Organization for Women to speak on abortion, and be asked by the varsity athletes to hear their concerns about mandatory drug testing. In every instance, the CSAO should know about the issue in advance, should advise the president to accept or decline the invitation, and should inform the president about what to say and what to avoid. This, of course, requires that the CSAO remain well informed about campus groups and issues. And if this is the president's first year, all these meetings should be arranged by the student affairs leader, in an effort to provide the president with a balanced yet positive set of public experiences with student groups.

Presidents, of course, have many constituents, and students are among the most important. But very few presidents have the time or inclination to make daily decisions concerning students, and they should not be expected to do so. When residence hall rent is raised, when a student is not admitted and a prominent alumnus calls to intervene, when a student has been expelled for cheating and wants to appeal, or when a student is in an accident, the president may need to be informed, but does not need to be involved. At times the CSAO has to serve as a buffer, receiving criticism and heat that various individuals and groups might have preferred to unleash on the president. This helps make it possible for the president to remain effective with respect to the larger issues the institution is facing. The CSAO's inability or unwillingness to assume this unpopular decision-making role may also send a signal to the president that the chief student affairs officer is not a strong member of the management team. If mutual trust and understanding have been established, presidents will not only respect CSAOs for assuming responsibility for difficult and controversial issues, but will also come to depend on them to do so. This may place the CSAO in an unpopular light with some students, of course, but this is part of the responsibility of the position.

Many of the issues faced by institutions are controversial, especially as viewed by the public. Because the president and the CSAO are both highly visible, some students may delight in finding ways to expose any inconsistency in their actions and statements. Complete agreement on all issues is obviously not possible, but it is the CSAO's responsibility to support the president. At times, an institutional decision may raise an ethical dilemma for CSAOs. For example, questions of fairness in admissions policies may be raised if a donor's child is given special consideration; questions of equal rights may be raised if a gay student organization is denied access to the homecoming parade; questions of freedom of expression may be raised if a student magazine is chastised for its racy poetry; or questions of justice may be raised if a politically bothersome but promising student is suspended for a minor conduct infraction. Such· situations inevitably occur in colleges and universities, and may test the relationship between the CSAO and the president. If the CSAO has worked diligently to inform and educate the president about such possible conflicts before they happen, then a mutual trust and respect may be formed that allow them to deal with these touchy issues in an ethical manner. Many of the problems experienced by CSAOs occur because there is no clear understanding with the president. If CSAOs are unsure of the president's support, they may lack the confidence or courage to act. Moreover, there is likely to be little consistency in decisions made, and the anxiety of these leaders will increase as they struggle to guess what may be acceptable at the time to their presidents. Such situations almost always result in embarrassment for the institution, poor policies for students, and eventually the resignation or termination of the CSAO.

Relationship to the Chief Academic Officer

The chief academic officer has responsibility for teaching, research, libraries, and other academic programs. The chief academic officer on most campuses has responsibility for the majority of the institution's budget, and among the vice presidents is generally considered to be the "first among equals." The CSAO's relationship to the chief academic officer is almost as important as the relationship to the president. If the CSAO and the chief academic officer have widely differing views about education and the role of the university in its relations with students, the separation between academic and student life will most likely be great. When Woodrow Wilson was president of Princeton, he argued that "so long as instruction and life do not merge in our colleges, so long as what the undergraduates do and what they are taught occupy two separate airtight compartments in their consciousness, so long will the college be ineffectual" (1925, p. 244). This essentially defines what the goal of the CSAO–chief academic officer relationship should be: working together for the education of students, so that the college experience is viewed as a whole.

Some writers (Brown, 1972; Rodgers, 1980; Knefelkamp, Widick, and Parker, 1978; Miller and Prince, 1976) have argued that student development (devoting effort to specific stages of students' growth) should be the focus of the student affairs program. But most experienced CSAOs, while sympathetic to the ideas of these student development advocates, have reacted unenthusiastically to any proposals for a separate curriculum, because they know such proposals could not succeed. Traditional academic officers are very unlikely to make radical changes in

the curriculum, especially when many student development proposals have been so filled with psychological jargon that they
do not seem credible. And some academic administrators and
faculty view the student development approach as an attempt
to establish a separate curriculum, isolated from the core institutional teaching program. Student affairs leaders also could
not support an approach that represented the exact opposite of
what they were working to accomplish: integration of academic
and student affairs, not separation. Moreover, it would be impossible for a CSAO to be a contributing member of the institutional management team while advocating what might be
perceived as a separate curriculum.

During the past ten years, there has been considerable
activity directed toward forming partnerships between academic
and student affairs (see Mitchell and Roof, 1988; Stodt and Klepper, 1987; Brown, 1989). In the recent calls for reform in undergraduate education, there has also been a strong emphasis
on involving students in all aspects of the institution and viewing all of students' experiences as related to their education (see
National Institute of Education, 1984; Boyer, 1987). The former reflects the efforts of CSAOs on many campuses to inte-
grate student and academic life, and the latter represents the
increasing concern with the fragmentation of undergraduate
studies.

The pioneering statement of educational philosophy in
the student affairs profession, *The Student Personnel Point of View*
(American Council on Education, 1937), was issued more than
fifty years ago; in 1987, another statement was written in com-
memoration of the golden anniversary of the original document.
The first assumption of *A Perspective on Student Affairs* is worth
noting here, for it represents the basis approach CSAOs should
take in their relationship with the chief academic officer: "The
academic mission of the institution is preeminent. Colleges and
universities organize their primary activities around the academic experience: the curriculum, the library, the classroom,
and the laboratory. The work of student affairs should not compete with and cannot substitute for that academic experience.
As a partner in the educational enterprise, student affairs en-

hances and supports the academic mission" (National Association of Student Personnel Administrators, 1987, pp. 9–10). Very little will be accomplished if the CSAO attempts to compete with the chief academic officer, or is not supportive of the major academic goals of the institution. Most important, both academic leaders need each other and can improve the institution's educational program by working together.

Chief academic officers are very likely to have been faculty members for many years, and then academic deans. They tend to remain in their positions about five or six years, and more than one-third report that they would like to become college or university presidents (Moden, Miller, and Williford, 1987). Chief academic officers may be physicists, sociologists, political scientists, or engineers, and of course their approach to their position reflects their academic backgrounds and interests. The CSAO should become familiar with this approach as soon as possible; in fact, when a new chief academic officer is hired, the student affairs leader should be an active participant in the search and interview process.

More generally, both administrators should make efforts to learn about the responsibilities, problems, and issues associated with the other. The CSAO should be well acquainted with the general education requirements in the various academic divisions, with all the deans and department chairs, and with significant numbers of influential faculty. The chief academic officer should know and understand the student affairs departments, should be able to work with key student leaders, and should be familiar with the major issues and problems faced by student affairs.

Many administrators have not worked directly with anyone in student affairs before their appointment as chief academic officers. Their views about students and student affairs may reflect something they read in the newspaper, or something they saw student affairs staff doing twenty years ago.

The chief academic officer may also not have much previous experience working with student organizations, and this presents the CSAO with an excellent opportunity to introduce him or her to various student groups. Then, when there are student complaints about such matters as class size, library hours, or computer access, the chief academic officer will be more effective in responding to these problems. He or she can also be very helpful to the CSAO by demonstrating support for campus policies and programs affecting students. All in all, it is the responsibility of the CSAO to inform the chief academic officer about the goals and purposes of the student affairs division and to convince this official that collaboration between academic and student affairs will be to the institution's benefit.

Almost every aspect of the two officers' responsibilities can be enhanced by cooperation and collaboration. Examples of activities that can be pursued jointly include institutional research; student assessment, recruitment, orientation, and retention; international education; child care; substance abuse education; honors programs; student publications; career and cooperative education; grants administration; multicultural programs; and volunteer and service activities. If the CSAO can enlist the support of the chief academic officer in these programs, their quality and credibility will certainly be enhanced. Failure to involve the chief academic officer in such efforts may result in isolation of student affairs activities, and may separate the CSAO from the management team concept.

Relationship to the Chief Financial Officer

The principal business or financial officer of the institution usually has responsibility for accounting, payroll, purchasing, personnel, employee benefits, the physical plant, parking, auxiliaries, security, and auditing (Hyatt and Santiago, 1986). The chief financial officer's influence is reflected throughout the institution, in the day-by-day business conducted in departments, in the physical appearance of the campus, in the way students and staff are treated in various offices, and in the way financial policies are applied to programs and activities. This officer is a key member of the institutional management team, and is very important to the success of the CSAO.

Chief financial officers view themselves as major participants on this team, and they want to be involved in campus programs and student life. It is the responsibility of the CSAO to see that this happens, and to see that it happens in a positive manner. The most effective initial way to get chief financial officers involved with student affairs is to introduce them to students. The student affairs leader can invite the chief financial officer to make a presentation at a student leadership conference, ask this officer to join the baseball team for an out-of-town trip, ask him or her to set up a financial education program for student organizations, or take the chief financial officer to dinner in residence halls to meet with students. After several such contacts, the chief financial officer will no doubt feel more comfortable with students, and will be amenable to further involvement in the student affairs program.

CSAOs must, of course, deal with such matters as violations of college rules and state laws, destruction of property, public demonstrations, and campus violence. The key to effective institutional programs and policies in each of these areas is usually a strong, trusting relationship between the CSAO and the chief financial officer. These difficult and highly visible problems require coordination and cooperation between the two administrators if the institution is to achieve any positive results. The CSAO is more likely to get the support of the chief financial officer in these critical problem areas if the CSAO has already been involved with students and student affairs. Chief financial officers are in a much better position to be of assistance after a campus sexual assault has occurred if they have already been part of campus student discussions about date rape and violence; they are more helpful in finding solutions to residence hall damage problems if they have spent actual time in the halls; and they are more likely to understand and support the security requirements at a major campus concert if they have previously spent time talking with student government leaders. It is the responsibility of the CSAO to convince the chief financial officer that such involvement is critical to the success of the institution. It represents one of the key ways these two major administrative officers work together as part of the management team.

CSAOs recognize that the quality of the student-institution relationship is a function of all the experiences students have in college. How students are treated by the police, how their complaints are handled when paying a bill, how they are received by secretaries and other support staff, and how seriously their ideas are considered may all have an influence on them. Such matters often have as much to do with retention problems and student satisfaction as academic concerns (Noel, Levitz, Saluri, and Associates, 1985; Astin, 1977). The chief financial officer has responsibility for many of the departments that can influence the quality of life on the campus, and the CSAO should work closely with him or her to encourage positive results. For example, the campus police may need special training to work effectively with foreign students; clerks in the bursar's office may need to show more sensitivity to Hispanic students; the parking office may receive fewer complaints if students were involved in setting campus parking policies. An alert CSAO will know about such concerns, and will work with the chief financial officer in addressing and correcting them.

The best chief financial officers, of course, are not just interested in responding to problems and correcting them, but in being part of a team effort to build an effective and humane institution. It is in this broad area where the most exciting and rewarding aspects of the relationship of the chief student affairs and financial officers can take place. These two major campus leaders can have a very positive influence on the "ecology of the campus" (Banning, 1989) by studying together the aspects of the total environment that affect student life. The design of buildings, the places where food is served, the informal areas constructed to encourage student-faculty contacts, and the places where students live are natural and necessary concerns of these two administrators. When chief financial officers are invited to become vital parts of the total education program of the campus, most of them will respond with enthusiasm.

The CSAO can also enlist the active involvement of the chief financial officer in making the campus as healthy and as safe as possible. The development of wellness programs at colleges and universities provides excellent opportunities for these two administrators to work together. With the great emphasis now being placed on campus safety, it is mandatory that these two administrators cooperate in this vital area as well. A decision to attend a national conference on campus safety together and then to formulate a plan of action for the institution may result in very positive outcomes. Both administrators need each other for success, and few programs are more important than campus safety in the 1990s.

CSAOs should have extensive financial management preparation and experience before assuming their positions. Such expertise is needed to administer the extensive programs and departments in the student affairs division, and to be an effective member of the institutional management team. If they take the position that fiscal matters are not their responsibility or offer the excuse that they have no accounting background, delegating these matters completely to someone on the staff, they will lose the respect of the chief financial officer, and perhaps the confidence of the president and other major administrators as well. But even with a good financial background, they are bound to encounter some problems. If CSAOs need assistance in developing fiscal policies, a close relationship with the chief financial officer will enable them to ask for help. A good working relationship with the chief financial officer will also help to ensure the fiscal integrity of student affairs programs. If funds are missing from the student government, if there is a rumor of any embezzlement in student financial aid, or if the billing procedures in the residence halls are generating student complaints, it is best to approach these problems from a common understanding between the CSAO and the chief financial officer. One of the basic assumptions of the management team approach is to help each other, not to compete with each other for the purpose of making someone else look bad. This can be a painful lesson for some CSAOs in fiscal matters, if they have been overly protective of "their" departments or fearful that assistance from the chief financial officer might result in a loss of control.

Relationship to the Chief Development Officer

Development has become one of the major functions of most colleges and universities in the past twenty years, and the chief development officer usually has the title of vice president or dean (Rowland, 1986). This administrative leader is a key member of the management team, and has responsibilities that include annual fund raising, capital campaigns, alumni affairs, and perhaps external and governmental relations (Pray, 1981). If the institution is national in scope, with very strong academic and professional programs, the development program may be organized in a decentralized manner, with staff in each of the major academic units. Even with such an arrangement, it is very likely that there will be a chief development officer for the university, functioning as part of the management team.

CSAOs should be expected to contribute to the success of the overall development program, and should work closely with the chief development officers to see that the student affairs division can benefit from development efforts. Successful institutional development programs are established through extensive planning and involvement of consultants, faculty, alumni, board members, and students. CSAOs can contribute to this process through their knowledge of the campus and of the special needs and problems of students. They should have extensive information about students' family backgrounds and hometowns. They should provide detailed reports about the postgraduation activities and locations of alumni, including data about major corporations and professional activities. CSAOs should be able to provide useful assessment data, indicating how students and alumni have reacted to their alma mater. They should be active participants in alumni programs, on and off campus, and should be expected to be part of direct solicitation efforts for the institution. CSAOs have responsibilities that are directly related to successful development programs, and thus their participation in them is essential.

CSAOs rarely have sufficient resources to address all of the needs they and their staff have identified. In the interviews conducted with CSAOs as part of this study, the search for resources was consistently identified as their most important and difficult task. Many now see the institution's development program as a very promising source of support.

The first lesson for student affairs leaders is that there is no "free lunch." Simply stating a need and asking for money from the chief development officer will not bring success. What is likely to succeed is a specific plan, supported primarily by student affairs staff members, that will benefit the institution as a whole — including the development office. For example, a proposal to start a parents' association was developed by the CSAO at the University of Virginia, and a specific plan was presented. The student affairs staff provided most of the personnel support, and the development office contributed its expertise and advice. Donations were shared, but most were dedicated to special orientation, advising, and counseling programs for students. This special development program at Virginia has been very successful, not only in providing extra funds to support student services, but also in establishing an effective link with parents of currently enrolled students. Indiana University has had similar success in attracting generous support for student leadership programs by soliciting alumni who were extensively involved in campus life as undergraduates. This was a joint project of the chief student affairs office and the development office. Responsibility for the placement function puts student affairs staff in contact with major corporations on a regular basis, and many of these organizations may provide support for special campus programs for students. The University of Florida has funded scholarships, fine arts programs, ethnic history displays, and a student lecture series from such sources. Close cooperation with the chief development officer on such efforts is essential, since there are almost always other fund-raising initiatives at the institution directed to those same corporations.

One of the most important contributions the CSAO can make to the institution's development and alumni program is to emphasize the importance of the quality of life for currently enrolled students. Asking alumni to support their alma mater is infinitely more successful if they were treated humanely as undergraduates, had stimulating and personal contacts with faculty, and were involved in student organizations. In fact, this is a fine opportunity for CSAOs to gain further support for student affairs. Providing effective support services for undergraduate students is essential to the success of the total educational program, but it may pay handsome financial dividends in the future as well.

Many CSAOs and chief development officers have worked together to establish student support groups or student foundations. If good planning has occurred, there is usually extensive student interest in this activity, and very able students can be selected. Such groups can represent the university at a variety of events, can serve as hosts and hostesses, can form student speaker bureaus, and can also participate in direct solicitation efforts. Perhaps most important, they can reinforce the value and importance of a long-term relationship with the institution.

At most large universities, each of the colleges (for example, medicine, business, or law) has its own development officer, and sometimes these staff members are jointly supported by the college and the chief development officer. Some student affairs leaders have done the same thing. Of course, this requires careful planning with the chief development officer, and enough previous success by the CSAO to justify the effort. Having a fund-raising staff person in the student affairs division may have special promise for development efforts targeted to specific capital projects for students, such as unions, residence halls, or recreation buildings. But CSAOs who are relatively new to development will probably achieve more success by collaborating with the development office. If considerable success is realized over a period of a few years, then a more ambitious program, housed in the student affairs division itself, may be justified.

CSAOs share a responsibility with other members of the management team in dealing with ethical issues. In the solicitation, receipt, and distribution of donated dollars, ethical dilemmas are sure to surface. Is it appropriate to accept money from organizations or individuals who have not conducted themselves ethically? Is it acceptable to approach a donor who is known to have bigoted racial views? Is it right to accept dollars designated by the donor for purposes that may contradict college admissions policies? CSAOs must have clearly thought through their own educational principles before assuming their positions, and must feel comfortable about the priorities of their institution. If they feel compelled to compromise their principles because of ethical dilemmas associated with the development program, then it is their responsibility to find a position at another institution.

3

Working with Students

CSAOs exist for the education of students. For this reason they are expected to be experts on the student body. This requires an in-depth understanding of the students, the ability to establish trusting relationships with them, responsiveness to student and staff problems and issues, and a willingness to take some risks. These are the major issues explored in this chapter.

Understanding Students

The president, the governing board, the alumni, the faculty, the community, and parents all expect the CSAO to be the expert on the students. But simply being appointed to this position does not magically confer any special understanding! How does the student affairs leader develop an accurate understanding of students, especially with the incredible diversity of student backgrounds at most colleges and universities? We will consider some of the more obvious strategies.

Listen to Many Groups. CSAOs receive a great deal of unsolicited advice from faculty, staff, alumni, parents, and community members about a wide variety of topics. They need to recognize that understanding their student body requires continual assessment and insight from these and other sources. It requires discipline and honesty as well as a willingness to listen, especially to facts and viewpoints that may not always be pleasant. Perhaps most important, it requires an open mind, as free as possible from preconceived notions about what the students are really like.

Use Available Data. The CSAO has access to a large amount of data about students, and he or she should take advantage of this. The admissions staff can provide information regarding test scores, high school grades, and demographics of student applicants. It is also extremely useful to accompany the admissions staff on some of their visits to schools. Face-to-face conversations with high school principals, counselors, and community leaders can frequently provide valuable insights into students' attitudes and background. In particular, it may help the CSAO understand the major reasons students are selecting the college, and what their perceptions and expectations are.

Know Students' Reasons for Attending or Not Attending the Institution. Most colleges attract only a portion of the students they admit, and understanding the reasons why certain students elect not to come may be at least as important to know as learning why others do come. To get reliable responses from these students is a challenge, but one the CSAO and the admissions staff should pursue vigorously. There may be perceptions regarding the curriculum, the residence hall environment, the level of tuition charges, or the nature of campus social life that act as a barrier for some students. Not having such information may be very detrimental to the institution, and may hamper the CSAO in gaining an accurate picture of the student body.

Consult with Campus Offices. A number of institutions invite high school counselors to the campus to meet with admissions officers and the students who have actually enrolled at the college from those high schools. Such conversations almost always yield valuable information about students, their experiences, and their academic and personal aspirations. CSAOs should not only encourage such interaction, they should also be direct participants in some of the discussions.

The financial aid office can provide critical information about students' financial backgrounds. The CSAO should expect the director of student aid to prepare annual profiles of the socioeconomic status of the student body, showing differences between groups of students by gender, race, residence, curriculum, and age. It is very important for the CSAO to know how many students are aid recipients, how many are employed, and what the average loan indebtedness of students may be at graduation. The CSAO is administratively responsible for the student financial aid office, but beyond this, it is important to know what financial pressures the students are experiencing in their daily lives at the college. Very few will do well in their studies, participate in campus activities, or view their college experience positively if they are constantly worried about money.

Use Assessment Services. A major reason for high attrition rates and unenthusiastic responses of students to campus programs is a fundamental misunderstanding of the student experience. CSAOs will not serve their institutions well by relying on anecdotal accounts of what students are like, what their aspirations are, and what their reactions to campus and academic life are. On the contrary, it is the responsibility of the CSAOs to see that rigorous and systematic assessments are made of students, and to use this information with other institutional leaders for the improvement of educational programs. Since this is one of the CSAOs' most critical functions, they must assure themselves that they are using reliable procedures to obtain information about students. They should explore the possible benefits of participating in a national assessment program, such as the Cooperative Institutional Research Program (Astin, 1987) of the American Council on Education. This enables them to view their students in relation to students at other institutions, and to discern, in a systematic manner, trends on a great variety of issues over a period of years. Information obtained from such assessments can be shared with other members of the institution's management team, academic deans, faculty, the governing board, and alumni. This information is often unsettling to faculty and other administrators, especially if the results seem critical of particular programs or do not conform with what student attitudes were assumed to be. But CSAOs need such data if they are to help their institutions build effective educational programs.

Listen to Parents. Another group of people who can help the CSAO understand students are parents. Many institutions have developed parents' programs, involving them in orientation, student life, and advising activities. A parents' advisory group may provide the CSAO with valuable insights about students that cannot be acquired from any other source. Moreover, parents' groups may evolve into support organizations, enabling the chief student affairs office to provide various services to students on the recommendation of the parents' group. Care must be taken to include parents in any such group from the broad spectrum of the student body.

Consult with Employers. The CSAO should listen to the placement director and representatives of major corporations who hire the institution's graduates. They will have many useful insights about students and their professional competencies and aspirations. Are the students viewed as having good social and communication skills? Are they viewed as lacking in leadership ability? Are they positive about their undergraduate majors? How do they perform in employment interviews? The CSAO should have good answers to all these questions, because this information is necessary to decide what programs and policies should be implemented to improve services for students.

Monitor Student Health. The CSAO can also obtain valuable data from the staff at the counseling center and the health service. What kinds of psychological and family-related problems are new students bringing to the campus? What is the level of stress being experienced, and to what extent are students acting out this stress in alcohol and drug abuse, poor study habits, or other self-defeating behavior? What health-related problems do students suffer from that reveal difficulties in the campus environment? Answers to these and other questions can shed light on the nature of services that should be offered. Student affairs leaders are responsible for the counseling and health services, but sometimes they do not take the time to have the staff describe the actual personal experiences of students at the institution. While the outward appearances of most traditional-age college students may be happy and healthy, the walking wounded are numerous on all campuses, and it is very important for the CSAO to have an accurate understanding of these problems. The president, the other vice presidents, and the faculty may be reluctant to accept such information, but they must be persuaded to accept it, since it is crucial to efforts to build a successful and humane academic program.

Learn About Student Life-Styles. More than others, student affairs leaders should know that all the experiences of students have a bearing on the success of the institution and that CSAOs should not confine themselves to dealing with major issues and problems. Students' living arrangements and eating habits may seem mundane, but it is important to know about them. These seemingly minor factors may influence students' choice of major, their attitudes toward the campus, their views on political and social issues, and their cultural sophistication. Discovering where and when students eat may reveal concerns for the college about health, costs, and isolation of students from faculty. Do the campus residence and dining facilities contribute to a sense of community, or do they further separate students from the college? Unless CSAOs actually visit these facilities and experience how students live on a daily basis, they really do not have a sufficient understanding of a very important part of student life.

Stay in Touch. Many CSAOs, especially those on large campuses, are very conscious of the dangers of isolating themselves from the reality of student life, relying only on office-based contacts with students or on what other staff members tell them. In the author's conversations with CSAOs, many reported that their formal associations tended to be with student leaders, or with other relatively visible and active students. This of course can create an unbalanced picture. Thus most of them indicated that in addition to relying on systematic assessment programs, they sought out students randomly in a wide variety of settings to listen to them talk about their campus experiences. Such contacts in the union bowling alley, the library, the recreation center locker room, or the local fast food restaurant certainly are not a scientific sample, but they often provide important insights about students that cannot be gained in any other way.

Consult with Academic Advisers. The staff responsible for academic advising in the colleges or departments on the campus are an excellent resource for student affairs leaders. What are student responses to the various curricula? Which are causing particular difficulties? How effective are faculty-student relations? Are there fair procedures in place for student academic appeals? What changes are the advisers noticing in the academic abilities and interests of students? Do minority students have any special academic concerns? CSAOs should have regular conversations with the academic advisers, since the answers to these questions are very important to policy and program planning.

Get into the Classroom. Despite their very demanding schedules, some CSAOs also teach one course per year, not only because doing so may keep them in touch with their academic discipline, but also to gain insights into the student experience that are not available in any other way. Even if only fifteen or twenty undergraduates are involved, teaching a class can remind the student affairs leader of what the classroom experience is like for students. However enjoyable and stimulating it may be, though, the CSAO must remember that it is a supplemental activity and should not be pursued if it interferes with major administrative commitments.

Understand Student Interests. The most sensitive CSAOs understand that it is very valuable to stay in touch with students regarding their political, religious, and aesthetic interests. This information is rarely accessible via official surveys or as a result of formal, office-based contacts; instead, CSAOs should rely primarily on their own interactions with students. This requires getting to know students well enough so that they are willing to share their thoughts and feelings in a candid manner. On most campuses, many points of view are represented, of course, but an awareness of general trends in student views can be very important in planning educational strategies and in developing successful cocurricular programs. If only a few students visit art galleries, attend plays, or go to the symphony, the CSAO should know this, and may want to use the knowledge to develop ways of increasing awareness. If there are strongly felt differences in the religious commitments of students, it is important for the CSAO to understand them, not just to avoid possible problems and conflicts, but to plan programs that can increase tolerance. If most students do not even bother to register to vote, and exhibit very little interest in political issues, the student affairs leader certainly should use this knowledge to initiate programs to encourage good citizenship.

Understand Special Student Communities. Perhaps the most difficult and most important responsibility of CSAOs is to understand the special needs and concerns of the various subgroups of students that exist on every campus. Without careful attention to the particular problems of these subgroups, many student affairs efforts will fail. Thus, when they are asked the question "What are the students like these days?", the most experienced CSAOs reply with a question of their own: "Which group of students at our institution are you referring to?" Even at small campuses, various groups of students view their academic and social experiences differently. What special needs do the commuter students have? Why don't the Chinese students attend any cocurricular events? Why have the students in the Catholic Student Association chosen to disaffiliate from student government? Why do so many Hispanic students choose not to live in campus residence halls? Why have no women students ever been elected as student body president or editor of the campus newspaper? Why are juniors and seniors in the engineering school using the counseling center in such large numbers? Why have gay students become so invisible in the last three years on campus? Why are most Jewish students attending the college across the state and not ours? Why is it that very few African-American students purchase food cards in the campus dining services program? Student affairs leaders need to probe deeply with their staff and others to understand these and many other special needs. Few CSAOs will have exact answers to all these questions, but inattention to such detailed efforts to understand the needs of special groups will certainly result in an unsuccessful student affairs program.

Establishing Trusting Relationships

It is very possible for CSAOs to be experts on the student body, and to understand the special needs of students throughout the institution, and yet to fail in their jobs. One sure way for this to happen is for the student affairs leader to fail to establish trust with students. If students do not have confidence and faith in the CSAO, all of the programs and policies in the student affairs division will suffer, and eventually the student affairs leader will have to leave. How does the CSAO establish this trust?

Be Honest. The one principle that takes precedence above all others in establishing trust with students is honesty. Students must know that they can consistently expect it from the CSAO. If the student affairs leader insists that there will not be a change in tuition and then tuition is increased by 10 percent, credibility is lost. If the CSAO promises residence hall student leaders that a new security alarm system will be installed and it does not happen, trust is eroded. If Hispanic students are told that a special scholarship program will be established to attract more students to the institution and this is not done, credibility is gone. CSAOs are expected to have answers, and often to give assurances to students that some program, policy, or service will be delivered. They must always be honest in their responses and careful not to mislead students into false expectations.

Even though it is frequently unpleasant for the CSAO to be honest with students (for example in informing them of a tuition increase), the consequences of being dishonest with them are far worse, not to mention being unethical. The position demands educators with strong personal integrity as well as the ability to withstand the consequences of being candid with students.

It is not just important for the CSAO to be honest with students in a general sense; it is critical to be honest all the time, on every issue or problem. More than one student affairs leader has run into trouble because of not being forthright on a relatively minor issue. It does not matter that the CSAO might have been honest with the students for years on all other problems — just one indication of failure to be honest can destroy years of efforts to establish trust with students. This Calvinistic standard can be very painful for CSAOs. But the student affairs leader may be the most visible administrator on the campus for the students, even more than the president. This constant visibility brings pressure from many groups, and requires that the CSAO be able to maintain integrity in the face of conflicting demands and considerable stress.

Demonstrate Personal Concern. CSAOs are engaged with very important educational issues and policies, are responsible for large budgets, and supervise many other professional staff members. However, this does not make much of an impression on students. If CSAOs see their role as essentially administrative, they will probably remain quite distant from students and have difficulty in establishing rapport with them. A more personal bond needs to be created. Honesty is not the only quality that is essential in winning the confidence and support of students; a genuine sense of caring is also necessary. Caring is expressed in many ways, of course. Public statements in the press and speeches made at banquets are important up to a point. But visiting sick students in the hospital, sending thank you notes to students for their good work, remembering the names of students, inviting students to dinner, going to a sorority house to provide support when a member has died, attending a touch football game, asking students for their recommendations on a campus issue, and attending initiation ceremonies for dozens of student organizations all speak much more loudly than public statements. In showing the concern, CSAOs should avoid displaying any political, religious, or other biases. They must genuinely care for students, regardless of their views or unorthodox life-styles. It may be difficult to give equal time and concern to the Young Republicans and Young Democrats, the football team and the drama club, the residence halls and the Greeks, and the architecture students and the accounting students, but a sincere effort must be made to do just that.

Be Consistent. It is difficult for student affairs leaders to establish trusting relations with students if these leaders' actions are inconsistent. This is especially true regarding enforcement and interpretation of policies. If institutional regulations are not applied equally to students and faculty, if some student groups are treated more leniently than others, or if sanctions are applied unevenly, students will quickly take note and will become very skeptical of anything the CSAO says or does. This is often a dilemma for student affairs leaders, since they do not always have exclusive institutional control over these matters. For example, alcohol policies may be more stringently enforced for students than they are for others at home football games. If this is the case, it is highly likely that the student government association and the campus newspaper will point out such hypocrisy. They will also expect the CSAO to explain the problem and correct it, and will certainly publicly chastise the student affairs leader for letting it happen in the first place. CSAOs speak officially for their institutions in such situations and will lose credibility and trust if they are dishonest or inconsistent with the students. This points up the interconnection of the CSAO with other members of the college management team, who have the same obligation as the student affairs leader to be honest and consistent with students.

Involve Students in Policy Decisions. Establishing trust with students can be enhanced considerably by involving them in policy and program development and implementation. If students understand the policies and programs, have some say in their content, and share a role in the implementation process, they may be more likely to accept them and to trust the administrators who have worked with them. It is the responsibility of the CSAO to see that this involvement occurs. But a prerequisite is to have the understanding and commitment of administrators, faculty, and especially student leaders. If the plan for involving students is really nothing more than an attempt to appease them by offering them token spots on policy boards, they will quickly realize that the plan is a sham, and the CSAO's credibility will be severely damaged. To gain their trust and acceptance, the student affairs leader should work jointly with them to develop the method by which students will be selected for the various policy groups. If they are hand picked by the administrative staff or faculty to serve, they certainly will not be viewed as representative, and again, trust will be undermined. The student involvement plan is more likely to work if some basic instruction is provided to the students selected for the various committees each year. They need to understand the history, role, and authority of each policy committee, the names and positions of the faculty members who serve on them, and how the meetings are conducted. The effectiveness of students serving on these committees can be advanced considerably by yearly training sessions conducted by the student affairs staff, and the process itself can reinforce trust for the CSAO.

Follow Through on Programs. If students have significant involvement in policy making and policies are changed without their participation or knowledge, they will become furious and lose any trust they have in the CSAO. This may become an issue for the CSAO in relations with the president and other members of the management team. For example, some students may have been arrested at a fraternity party and charged with rape, causing great anger in the community and terrible embarrassment for the university. The CSAO may be under considerable pressure to bypass the process that was established by a student-faculty committee a year ago to adjudicate such cases and simply to suspend the fraternity immediately. However, if this is done, the students who participated in the policy-making body, as well as those now serving on the implementation committee, will feel their work was in vain. The CSAO must be committed to the idea of student involvement and must be willing to live with its consequences, both positive and negative. There is really no middle ground on this issue. Consistent follow-through can greatly enhance the trust that students have for the institution. But if policy making is a sham, it will be quickly revealed as such by the students and will fail. Even worse, it will result in a great loss of faith in the integrity of the CSAO on the part of students.

Maintain Confidences. CSAOs are administrators, not practicing psychologists or counselors. However, they encounter a good deal of information about students that must be kept confidential. If trusting relations with students are to be developed and maintained, students must have confidence that matters they share with the CSAO will not be disclosed to others. If they do not have this assurance, they will not seek assistance and will become very resentful toward those in charge. Information about student suicides, the names of students who have been disciplined, or the grades of student athletes are often vigorously sought by the press. The CSAO should have in place policies and procedures that anticipate such requests and should reevaluate them periodically. While no system is leakproof, it is the student affairs leader's responsibility to see that the policies and procedures are well known to the campus community and that they are enforced daily. Besides the legal obligations involved, the credibility and trust of the institution and the CSAO are at stake.

Set an Example. Policies, programs, and formal committees are important in establishing trust with students, but CSAOs should never forget that their personal relationships with students and faculty will ultimately determine how much trust they earn. While they are certainly not expected to be saintly, they are highly visible to students and must recognize that they live in a fishbowl. Only the president's behavior is usually subject to more scrutiny, both on and off campus. Some CSAOs, in their zeal to establish trust with students and gain their support, have become too familiar with them and have lost their respect as a result. Students do not want or need CSAOs to be their close friends; they do, however, deserve student affairs leaders whose integrity and personal concern they can admire. If CSAOs "pay their dues" over time, by working with students, getting to know them, sharing their concerns with them, admitting their own mistakes, and being honest with them, a level of trust can develop that will enable them to accomplish a great deal. CSAOs must develop the same kind of relationship with faculty, for without their confidence and support, students may view the student affairs staff with disdain. If student affairs leaders are openly critical of the lack of faculty participation in student life, it will do little to build support for student affairs and may cause students to wonder about the respect campus professionals have for one another. And students and faculty have to know the CSAO as a person, not just as an administrator, if a high level of trust is to be achieved. If they do not trust CSAOs or think they are too distant and impersonal, they will find many ways to see that their ideas and proposals fail.

Responding to Student and Staff Issues

CSAOs face many difficult and complex problems in their relationships with students. How well they handle them has a major impact on their effectiveness. It is very important for CSAOs to understand the distinctive character of their own campuses and the expectations students, faculty, and other administrators have of them. They also need to think carefully about their role as administrators, and to learn when, where, and how to exert their influence.

At many colleges and universities, especially larger ones, a dean of campus life reports to the CSAO. This dean is usually responsible for administering the campus judicial system. The CSAO must be careful not to usurp the role of the campus life dean, or the students will learn to bypass the dean's office and will expect the CSAO to make all the important decisions. The CSAO may be tempted to intercede in other areas as well, such as housing, financial aid, and admissions, because of the frequency, visibility, and sensitivity of the problems involved. Doing so too often, though, may undermine the authority and confidence of staff members in those areas and send confusing messages to students. Among the best ways to circumvent the problem is to hire excellent staff and then to allow them to function as professionals. The students will then understand that the officials in charge of student life, housing, financial aid, and admissions have the authority to act in their own right, and so they will be seen as significant campus leaders.

Allow Students to Follow Through. To what extent should CSAOs serve as advocates of students? When should student organizations and student themselves assume this role? This is

an issue that often tries the patience of CSAOs. Most know that
they can present proposals to the campus community with better timing, greater depth, and more persuasiveness than students can. They are also usually aware of the flaws in the processes and content of student proposals, and may be anxious
about losing support for a new program or project because of
them. On the other hand, they know the value of the learning
that can take place when students themselves see a project
through to completion. If CSAOs never permit students to become their own advocates, the students are unlikely to develop
very effective leadership skills and may not feel any ownership
for what happens on their campus. An overly aggressive or re-
strictive CSAO may erode the confidence the students think the
student affairs leader has in them, and this may eventually result
in resentment and lack of support. Advocacy for student needs
is a major role for a CSAO, but sensitivity to the students themselves in knowing when to exercise this advocacy must be demonstrated. Students may not want the CSAO as their primary advocate on all issues they propose, but it is likely that they will
expect some moral support or "quiet cheerleading" from the sidelines. Of course, there will be times when student proposals will
be in direct opposition to what the students know the CSAO
supports. The student affairs leader should openly acknowledge
these differences of opinion, while at the same time helping the
students understand the process by which institutional decisions
are made.

Be Sensitive to the Needs of Other Offices. CSAOs may face a
delicate issue when students present grievances to them about
the poor behavior of faculty, staff, or other administrators. Students will expect action to correct what they feel is a serious
problem. How CSAOs respond may have a major influence on
how well they are accepted by students and respected by other
staff and faculty. Unless the person being complained about is
a member of the student affairs staff, the CSAO may not be
able to effect a change, even if the students' grievance is justified.
But the CSAO should not ignore the student complaint or simply refer it to someone else to avoid having to deal with it. In

many cases, student affairs leaders can initiate actions to correct the problem because they have previously established good relationships with staff and faculty and are trusted by them to handle problems in a professional manner. This again illustrates how important it is for CSAOs to develop trusting relations with faculty and other campus administrators in order to establish good relationships with students in turn.

Balance Crises and Student Programs. Student affairs leaders spend a good deal of their time reacting to student problems and crises, because it is impossible to predict or control all aspects of campus life. When a student suicide occurs, when a major student protest takes place, or when there is a fire in a residence hall, everything else becomes secondary and the CSAO's attention is directed to the immediate problem. Some CSAOs may define their jobs as crisis management and thus reinforce the common notion on some campuses that all student affairs administrators are for is to put out student fires. Constantly responding to student crises, and then dramatizing them to colleagues, may give the most insecure CSAOs a feeling of importance. They may even neglect their real responsibility, which is to develop high-quality student life programs in support of the academic goals of the institution. The best CSAOs cannot escape the obligation to respond to student crises, of course, but they do not allow themselves to become permanent captives of such problems. Moreover, if students see CSAOs only in crisis-related situations, the resulting stereotype will make positive program development very difficult. But all student affairs leaders must face the difficult challenge of balancing crisis management of student problems with their primary responsibilities for developing quality student life programs. Failure to find an effective balance may result in poor relations with students and negative views of the effectiveness of the chief student affairs officer.

Establish Fair Policies. On almost every campus, there are dozens of student organizations addressing a great variety of issues and problems facing higher education and society as a whole. As a result, the CSAO will encounter some difficult and delicate issues. A fraternity has a party with a racially insulting theme; a student group preaches white supremacy; a student publication includes sexually demeaning photographs of women; the student government refuses to provide funding support for the Gay Student Alliance; the premedical student society distributes free condoms to students and parents at orientation; and the campus newspaper wants to publish information about the personal financial investments of the president. How CSAOs approach such issues with students and student organizations has a significant impact on their effectiveness and on how they are perceived by students and faculty. If student affairs leaders respond to student organization problems without regard to any previously developed policies, they will certainly encounter trouble. Principles such as freedom of expression, the right to assemble, sensitivity to diversity, and respect for privacy must be discussed in detail, and should form the basis for a comprehensive institutional policy on student activities. It is the responsibility of the CSAO to see that this happens, and to ensure that the resulting guidelines are enforced fairly. Such policies should reflect the distinctive character and purposes of each institution. No policy can provide a prescription for every awkward or sensitive problem students might invent, but in the absence of any values-based policy, the CSAO will be hard pressed to develop consistent, trusting relations with students.

Respond to Students with Sensitivity. What responsibility for student welfare does the CSAO have when students' problems or grievances are not part of the administrative purview of the student affairs division? Most students do not care about division of labor reflected in university organizations when they have problems; they simply want them solved, and so they go to whoever they think can solve them. Very often, this is the student affairs staff. Even when the problems presented by students are unrealistic and outside the jurisdiction of their divisions, student affairs leaders should try to respond in humane and sensitive ways. Failure to do so may affect their ability to maintain trusting relations with students on issues they can affect.

Of course, CSAOs want students to view them as being

very responsive to their problems, but what happens when the results are not what the students sought? Student affairs leaders cannot change academic requirements, federal financial aid laws, the prices local merchants charge for their goods, or the decisions made by the city council. Yet all experienced student affairs administrators have met with many students who expect them somehow to work such miracles. CSAOs can defuse criticism for their failure to solve specific problems through their broader contributions to the university and the community. After all, even students who may not be highly involved in campus life programs are often quite aware of the personal and professional actions of highly visible institutional leaders. These actions usually affect students' perceptions of CSAOs more than anything they say. If they see their CSAO speaking publicly for their rights as citizens in the community, appearing before a legislative committee on behalf of child-care needs, or chairing the citywide school volunteer program, they will take notice and will realize that this administrator is a leader whose actions off the campus support the values stated on the campus.

Treat All Students Equally. Student affairs leaders may discover that the great majority of their student contacts are with a few campus leaders. This poses another dilemma for them in their relations with students: How can the CSAO be responsive to the students who are campus organization leaders and at the same time reach out to the large numbers of students who are uninvolved? It takes long hours and hard work to develop and maintain good relations with student leaders, but if student affairs administrators ignore others, students may think they have to be campus big shots before they get any attention. The best CSAOs develop very sensitive "antennae" to the needs of uninvolved students, and make special efforts to seek them out. This can be done even on a large campus, and such efforts demonstrate to all students the sincere desire of the CSAO to address their concerns, not just those of the campus leaders. This approach can also demystify the office for students who do not normally visit administrators, and on the whole will humanize the institution for students.

Be Forthright About Substance Abuse. Student affairs leaders receive an abundance of advice regarding alcohol and substance abuse among students. They are expected to be well informed on the subject, tuned in to the realities of campus life, and in control of a campus judicial system designed to prevent abuse and rehabilitate the offenders. While the majority of traditional-age college students are under twenty-one, most of them consume alcohol, and most CSAOs report that by far the most serious behavioral problem on their campuses is alcohol abuse. How student affairs leaders handle this very difficult issue with students, parents, the president, and the governing board will affect their relationships with students and their effectiveness as administrators. CSAOs must take the lead in this entire process, not just to obtain a workable policy, but more important, to maintain good and trusting relations with students. Their approach to the campus alcohol issue can influence the way they are viewed by students more than anything else they do. If they take a rigid, distant, and authoritarian approach, it may satisfy some external pressure groups, but it will most likely result in failure. The students will deeply resent being treated like children, may turn against the institution, and may resort to all kinds of creative actions to subvert the policy. The main loser is usually the CSAO, who incurs the wrath and distrust of students. Thus CSAOs must take the lead in gaining the cooperation and participation of students in developing campus alcohol policies that recognize existing laws and institutional rules. Citizens under twenty-one do not enjoy any special immunity from state laws because they are college students or because they reside on a campus. If an alcohol policy is developed with a respect for student ideas, and if the students become convinced that the institution is sincere about working with them, then the policy has a chance to succeed.

Show Sensitivity to Student Stress. Students may appear to those who do not know them well to be healthy, happy, and carefree, but the college experience can in fact be a very stressful time, because of academic competition, career decisions, poor health habits, or personal and family relationship problems. CSAOs should work to develop their own special sensitivity to this critical problem by carefully observing students and investigating the major sources of stress they face. CSAOs should try to create a supportive campus climate where students are encouraged to seek assistance for their personal problems without feeling as if the institution is judging them. When the CSAO reaches out to students who are experiencing pain or stress, it will be appreciated and will demonstrate the college's genuine concern for student welfare. On the other hand, if the CSAO appears oblivious to the personal problems of students, a significant portion of the student body will conclude that he or she is ineffective and insensitive.

Being Willing to Take Risks

CSAOs recognize when they accept their positions that they are entering very risky territory. They are very visible, and with so many diverse constituencies to serve and so many decisions to make, it is impossible to escape controversy. Their willingness or refusal to take risks as administrators will inevitably be noticed by students and others.

Show Courage. The CSAO's job does not simply consist of applying certain policies and procedures. The person who occupies the position cannot hide behind a set of bland rules or bureaucratic red tape if anything significant is to be accomplished. Students and others will quickly recognize the overly timid or cautious CSAO and will respond to this official with disdain. The CSAO is constantly faced with controversy and should learn to accept this situation and use it effectively to influence students' education.

Speak Out on Issues. Student affairs leaders are members of the management team, but they will not gain much respect from students if they are silent on critical issues. Their silence will often be viewed as weakness or as an unwillingness to take a stand on an important problem. The president, the board, and some faculty members may grow a bit uncomfortable with a

CSAO who always seems to be stirring things up, but they should recognize that the institution and its students are not served well by having bland "yes-persons" in the position.

Motivate and Challenge. CSAOs are not just administrators of policies; they have a critically important role to inspire, to motivate, to challenge, and to love students. This is a position that should attract the most compassionate of educators — leaders who can, by personal example, gain the respect and affection of students. Students demand a real person with real attitudes and values in the CSAO position, and part of the challenge in becoming accepted by the students is to let them know clearly and forcefully where one stands. The position requires a strong person with firm educational commitments who is willing to share these commitments openly. The CSAO will not always be the students' champion; some public stands taken by this campus leader will be viewed negatively by students. It is more important to be heard and understood clearly than it is to be silent or popular.

Confront Controversy Openly. CSAOs may be at odds with others regarding their role with students. Some people may think that student affairs leaders are doing a good job if there is no visible turmoil. But achieving a harmonious campus or keeping things quiet has never been the goal of the best CSAOs. There are many difficult and important issues students should be engaged with on any campus, and no student affairs leader serves students or the institution well by trying to avoid them or by pretending they are not there. Thus student affairs leaders have a responsibility to raise issues, identify problems, and tackle delicate matters. Whether the issues are in politics, religion, health, or education, the students deserve a CSAO who is active and visible, challenging them to learn and to get involved. Students will not learn to be effective leaders if they have not dealt with controversy; racial and ethnic attitudes will not improve if students are not challenged and confronted; and students will not develop a sense of social conscience if they have been protected from other injustice and inequities during college. The educational arena occupied by student affairs is often messy, public, and controversial, and the CSAO should be an active and visible part of it.

CSAOs should not, of course, push their own personal biases on political or religious issues, but it is their responsibility to see that students are confronted with a variety of views on important social issues. This should be done even if some turmoil results from the process, which it usually does. CSAOs must recognize that the position is filled with risks; moreover, they must accept the fact that they are vulnerable to losing their jobs because of these risks. However, the best among them know that it is just these risks that can result in learning for students, and that can make their positions so challenging and rewarding.

4

Responding
to Campus, Community,
and Alumni Interests

During my conversations with chief student affairs officers, most described the diverse and often conflicting constituencies with which they regularly interact. The groups they most frequently mentioned were the faculty, the community, parents, the governing board, the legislature and the federal government, donors and alumni, and the student affairs staff. To be successful, CSAOs must cultivate positive relationships with each of these groups and earn their support as well. This is usually a complicated task, because of the inevitable differences among the various groups and the varying expectations some of them have for the student affairs leader. The most successful CSAOs have developed specific strategies to deal effectively with these major constituencies, and understand that their continued support is essential. Substantial antagonism from just one of these groups will not only hinder the actions of student affairs leaders; it can lead to their dismissal. This chapter discusses each of these groups and presents suggestions for establishing successful relationships with them.

The Faculty

Faculty members are the heart of the college, and on most campuses, the ratio of faculty members to professional student affairs

58

staff is at least fifteen to one. Through traditional campus governance structures, faculty members have a major role in establishing institutional policies and priorities. Thus, to suggest that much can be accomplished in student affairs without their support is foolhardy. CSAOs need to nurture good relations with the faculty, ensure that they are well informed about student affairs issues, and persuade them to be active participants in student life. This is one of the most important responsibilities of student affairs leaders, and one of the most challenging as well.

Some CSAOs have served as full-time faculty members earlier in their careers, and this experience may make them more confident in their work with the faculty. Many CSAOs also have a faculty appointment in an academic department as part of their contract with the institution. This arrangement may be helpful to student affairs leaders in their relations with the faculty, since they may more readily be received as academic colleagues. But such previous experiences or assignments do not guarantee success in establishing good faculty relations. CSAOs must demonstrate competence at what they do and earn the respect and support of the faculty on that basis. Faculty members will respond positively to student affairs leaders who work hard to improve learning opportunities for students and who show a genuine and professional concern for them.

Recognize Faculty Members. While faculty members may enjoy informal, out-of-class contacts with students, they do not get much encouragement to engage in such activities at most colleges and universities. The reward system generally favors research and publication, which makes the job of attracting faculty to student affairs activities even more challenging. The CSAO should work with the chief academic officer and the president to find ways that faculty members can be rewarded for their student life participation. This advocacy role by the student affairs leader is likely to be appreciated, and if successful, may pay rich dividends in the quality of student life over a period of years. Many CSAOs have established faculty recognition programs of their own, as a way of thanking those who have made significant contributions to student life. When faculty members are so recognized, their department heads, deans, and the chief academic officer can be invited to the program, and by their presence confirm the commitment of the institution to the value of faculty support for student life. The CSAO can also suggest that the outstanding teaching awards most colleges present to faculty include similar recognition for support of student life.

Become Visible with the Faculty. CSAOs must become very visible to faculty members through the institution. A good place to start is at the annual orientation meetings of new faculty members, where the student affairs leader can describe the division's programs and services and can suggest ways the new faculty appointees can become involved in student life. The CSAO should become a regular participant in the academic dean's council, and in the faculty senate as well. Such involvement can lead to positive relations with faculty members, and can open up new opportunities for their participation in student life. The faculty senate is likely to have a number of standing policy committees, and CSAOs and their staffs should be active participants in several of them. Senate committees on admissions and financial aid policy, student conduct, athletics, and placement are examples of faculty groups with which the student affairs leaders should become involved. There may also be a senate committee on student affairs, which may serve as a "faculty oversight" group for the division. The CSAO should get to know all the faculty members on these committees very well, should provide them with extensive information about services and programs, and should invite them to student events and student affairs meetings throughout the year. If the CSAO does not win the confidence of the faculty members from the various senate committees, it is very possible that the entire student affairs program may come under attack by these committees, which will place the CSAO in a precarious and defensive position. This is why the best CSAOs take a very aggressive approach to faculty senate committees dealing with student life issues, actively seeking their advice and assistance on relevant problems and programs. Student affairs leaders must again demonstrate competence in handling problems and delivering effective programs and policies that meet institutional needs. There is no substitute for this high level of competence; if CSAOs make fine-sounding speeches at the faculty senate month after month but do not produce effective results, credibility will diminish rapidly.

Communicate Clearly. In their work with the faculty, especially with formal academic policy committees, some CSAOs have hindered their own effectiveness by the excessive use of jargon. In an apparent effort to impress faculty members that they, too, represent an academic discipline with its own sophisticated language, some student affairs leaders have so obscured their messages that they have not only lost their audience but their credibility as well. It is the responsibility of the CSAO to communicate the goals of student affairs to faculty in a clear and persuasive manner. Failure to do so will greatly hinder what the entire student affairs staff can accomplish on the campus.

Use Faculty Members as Resources. CSAOs should recognize that they have the greatest resources imaginable for establishing effective student life programs: the faculty members on their own campus. Any college or university has experts on almost every issue and problem, and this expertise is there for the asking. If the CSAO needs advice or help on child care, student stress, wellness programs, drug and alcohol abuse, student assessment, legal issues, student health insurance, marketing strategy in admissions, leadership development, or just about any other topic, there are specialists on the faculty who can help. Indeed, it is in this area where student affairs leaders can probably benefit more from good faculty relations than any other. The CSAO should know more faculty members than anyone else on the student affairs staff, and should be familiar with their areas of special interest. Some student affairs staff conduct regular professional interest surveys of the faculty, cataloging the resources available to them and to student organizations. Once collected, such listings can prove very valuable in a search for the best advice available. Most faculty members are quite willing to help when asked to participate in a specific project related to their area of professional expertise.

Request Their Assistance. Most colleges and universities have large numbers of student organizations, and most require that each student group have a faculty adviser. This sometimes becomes difficult for student organizations, since some faculty may be reluctant to contribute the time required, especially if the group is associated with a controversial issue or is engaged in activities that may subject the group to liability claims. It is the duty of the CSAO to develop institutional policies that clearly describe the responsibility of faculty advisers to student organizations, and to define what their relationship is to the university. This, of course, will require the assistance of the institution's legal counsel, but the CSAO must take the lead in assuring the faculty who serve as advisers to student organizations that they can engage in this activity without undue fear or personal liability. This is especially important for student affairs leaders, since one of their tasks is to recruit good faculty members to serve as advisers to student groups and to convince them that such activity is worthwhile and enjoyable.

Match Faculty Members with Student Needs. As the primary expert on the diversity of the student body, the CSAO should be very sensitive to the needs of special groups of students. The student affairs leader should also be an expert on the faculty, and should serve as a matchmaker between special student groups and able faculty members who can be of help to them. CSAOs and their staff should know who might be especially well suited and inclined to provide support for handicapped students, students from different countries, minority students, students who have had a death in the family, students with behavioral problems, or students interested in studying abroad. There are never enough student affairs staff members to meet all the needs that students have on any campus, and it is the responsibility of the CSAO to know and identify faculty who can provide support for students. Such efforts can greatly extend the student affairs program on the campus, and can also convince faculty that the CSAO is genuinely concerned about students and is reaching out in effective ways to serve them.

Provide Useful Information. The student affairs leader can also enhance relations with faculty members by providing them with
periodic reports about students and campus issues. Reliable information about applicants, the composition and academic credentials of the student body, dropout rates and reasons for leaving, graduation rates and postgraduation activities, shifting
interests in academic majors, and student attitudes on various
issues can be shared with the faculty, and can become a basis
for policy and program discussions on the campus. There are
now lively debates among faculty members at most colleges about
the content and the organization of undergraduate education,
and the CSAO should be part of such discussions. If good information about students has been provided by the student affairs
division to the faculty over a period of time, it will seem natural
and necessary for the CSAO to be a part of curricular debates.

Recognize Differences in Institution Size. CSAOs in all institutions must work hard to win faculty support for student affairs,
but their strategies will differ in large and small colleges. CSAOs
working at small colleges probably know most of the faculty by
name, and the faculty members themselves are likely to interact with each other more frequently because departmental bound-
aries are not very tightly drawn. Relationships are informal,
and because faculty members are well known to students as well,
their participation in campus life is usually taken for granted.
The CSAO is able to get the attention of most of the faculty,
since there is good participation in campuswide governance
groups. At large universities, faculty are more remote and may
spend almost all of their time within their own department, rarely
focusing on institutional issues or even knowing students outside
of their own academic disciplines. As a result, CSAOs in large
universities must take the initiative to meet faculty members,
inform them about campus needs, and persuade them that their
participation in program and policy development is worthwhile.

Support the Chief Academic Officer. With the exception of the
president, the chief academic officer is usually the CSAO's closest

administrative colleague on the campus. Very little can be accomplished in establishing good relations between faculty and student affairs if the CSAO does not work well with the chief academic officer. If these two institutional leaders share trust, understanding, and similar goals, a great deal can be done. It is the responsibility of the CSAO to educate the chief academic officer about student life, and to demonstrate how cooperative efforts with the faculty can enhance the quality of education for all students.

Other than the students themselves, the faculty is the most important constituency for the CSAO in building support and understanding for the student affairs division. The entire student affairs staff should work closely with faculty members in efforts to get them involved with student life, but it is the CSAO who must take the lead in seeing that this happens. The campus functions best as a community, not as a group of separate, non-communicating administrative fiefdoms, and the CSAO should assume a major role in bringing faculty and student affairs together for the benefit of students.

The Community

The communities in which colleges and universities are located vary a great deal, of course, depending primarily on population. Miami University, with 15,000 full-time residential students, is located in Oxford, Ohio, a rural town of 5,000 residents. Emory University, with 5,000 students, is located in downtown Atlanta, a major urban center. Arizona State University, with over 40,000 students, is located in a metropolitan area of almost a million residents. Broward Community College enrolls over 30,000 students at four locations on the highly urban South Florida coast. Each of these institutions has its own special relationship with its community. The students are the most visible components of the institution from the community's point of view, and thus the CSAO has a special obligation to be an active participant in community affairs. What is the nature of this obligation, and how should the student affairs leader establish good relations with the community?

Support the President. Community relations are very important to the institution, and the CSAO should be well aware of the president's priorities in this area before initiating any specific programs or actions. The president and other members of the management team need to be informed in advance of any efforts the CSAO may want to make with the community. There may be an administrator assigned specific responsibility for community and government relations, and if this is the case, the CSAO should work closely with this person to develop good contacts and involvement. Thus the CSAO should support the president and remain sensitive to the goals of the institution within the community.

Know Community Leaders. The student affairs leader should initiate personal contacts with key community officials, such as the mayor, city council members, school board members, the city manager, the police chief, the fire chief, and members of the chamber of commerce. CSAOs should be on a first-name basis with all of these persons, who need to understand the composition of the student body, major problems and issues that can affect the community, and future plans for the institution. While the president is the most visible university official in the community, CSAOs should establish sufficiently strong relations with community leaders over a period of time that these leaders naturally turn to them when they have a concern related to students. Many CSAOs feel so strongly about the importance of good community relations that they have become directly involved as community leaders themselves. Some have been chamber of commerce presidents, fund-raising chairs for philanthropic groups, board members of volunteer agencies, and policy advisers to other organizations.

Prepare for Crises. One of the major reasons for CSAOs to become actively involved with the community is to be ready to respond to crisis situations. Fires, riots, and crime are not pleasant to deal with, but student affairs staff are expected to handle such matters, which almost always involve the community. The student affairs leader needs to work out the details of a coordinated institution-community response policy before such problems occur. The failure to establish such cooperative plans or the inability to implement them on a timely basis can lead to bitter criticism from community leaders and campus presidents. CSAOs cannot accomplish these tasks by staying on campus. They must be regular visitors to the offices of community officials, and they need to attend the formal and informal gatherings of community groups as often as possible. Through their presence, statements of concern, and ability to respond to problems effectively, CSAOs can earn the confidence and support of community leaders.

Promote Positive Relations. No one's interests are served when there is antagonism between students and the community. By interacting visibly with community business leaders, CSAOs can do a great deal to promote positive relations. Students have a major economic impact on the community, and the student affairs leader should represent the needs and rights of students with local business officials. But CSAOs can only do this well if they have established trusting relations with the business community over time. If they only appear at meetings once a year, do not know the names of local business leaders, or only attend a chamber of commerce meeting when they want something done for them, they cannot expect to be successful in community relations. Student affairs leaders can significantly improve relations with business leaders by inviting them to various campus events, especially those involving students. Many business leaders can contribute in substantial ways to student groups as advisers, seminar leaders, or project consultants. CSAOs should encourage such activity.

Build Joint Programs. In many communities, cooperative efforts between the CSAO and business leaders can open doors for significant student opportunities that benefit both the university and the community. The CSAO should be aware of federal and state programs designed to create jobs for students in the community, since these programs offer an ideal way to enhance relations and provide real benefits to students. CSAOs and their staff should also initiate contacts with the local community volunteer agencies and set up cooperative arrangements with student organizations interested in such participation. The city-university volunteer service link can be the most beneficial aspect of a program to work positively with the community. Everyone can benefit, and the students can learn values that are supportive of their classroom work.

Help Prevent Problems. At most colleges and universities, a substantial portion of the students live in the community, in many cases in apartment complexes built specifically to attract them. When large numbers of students are involved in such living arrangements, it is inevitable that landlord-tenant problems, security and crime, alcohol and drug abuse, and loud, late-night parties will become issues. The institution can choose to disassociate itself from such problems, claiming that they are not within the university's jurisdiction. But CSAOs know that such an approach cannot work, and if tried, will have a very negative impact on campus-community relations. If the student affairs leader does not initiate some actions with business and community leaders and apartment owners to address the problems, it is quite likely that students will be pitted against apartment owners in prolonged and often nasty disputes. If the CSAO has already established credibility with local business leaders and has the confidence of students, he or she can negotiate cooperative policies and procedures that can effectively and fairly serve the needs of both the apartment owners and the students. This is one of the most delicate aspects of campus-community relations for CSAOs to handle, and one of the most important as well. The student affairs leader must have good political skills to accomplish positive results, and needs the support of other members of the management team in the process.

Enhance Community Life. A much more pleasant community responsibility for CSAOs is their relationship to religious and cultural groups. By building positive relations with officials in these areas, student affairs leaders can enhance the quality of life and education for students and cultivate additional support services for the campus. Most churches and synagogues in college communities have professionals specifically assigned to work with students, and CSAOs and their staff should be well acquainted with all these persons. They can make very positive contributions to student life, and if they feel part of the campus community, they can greatly augment the overall student affairs program. Many of them also have excellent physical facilities, which can be used in cooperative programs between the student affairs staff and the religious advisers. If the CSAO has initiated actions that can build positive relations with local religious leaders, then it will seem natural to involve them in addressing such difficult campus issues as racial and ethnic tensions, ethical and moral problems, and AIDS education.

Know Special Community Groups. Student affairs leaders must also be aware of the many communities that exist within their cities. They should make efforts to get to know the most influential leaders of these various ethnic, racial, political, and religious groups. In responding to various problems on the campus, or in seeking ways to assist certain students, they will find good contacts with these special groups within the community essential. For example, if a Japanese-American student dies, the institution can demonstrate its concern and show its support much more effectively if the CSAO and key staff members have good relations with the Japanese community in the city. This sensitivity to the needs and concerns of specific communities is the responsibility of the student affairs leader.

Enrich the Quality of Life. Depending on the location of the college, the quality of the cultural life available to students may vary significantly. If the institution is in a cosmpolitan area, rich with art, music, dance, and theater, the CSAO may want to negotiate special opportunities for students. In communities that have very few cultural opportunities, the student affairs officer may want to suggest ways that the campus and community leaders can work together to enrich the quality of life for everyone. Such efforts, when successful, can enhance the learning of society and can become a source of pride for the community. Some student affairs administrators have special talents in this area and are active leaders in helping to bring the performing arts to their communities.

Establish Trust. Even with a CSAO who is aggressive, politically astute, and friendly with community leaders, it is inevitable that there will be tensions and strong differences of opinion in campus-community relations regarding students. For example, the student government association may implement a boycott of a local business; the student newspaper may enrage city boosters by calling the city council racist in an editorial; a fraternity party at a local hotel may result in extensive damage; late-night concerts on campus may anger local residents with loud noise; or plans for a new on-campus residence hall may be declared "unfair competition" by local apartment owners. Presidents expect CSAOs to handle these difficult problems and to solve them in ways that get as little publicity as possible, without endless committees and study groups. CSAOs often walk a tightrope between students and local business leaders, and it requires considerable skill to settle problems to everyone's satisfaction. They must be able to withstand some criticism from students as well as from community leaders, as they strive to meet the needs of both groups. The only way student affairs leaders can be successful in such efforts is if they have previously established a high level of trust and familiarity with the community, and of course with students. They must understand that establishing this trust is an essential part of their jobs, and that successful community relations can lead to good learning opportunities for students and benefits for the institution.

Parents

At colleges with traditional-age students, parents will be heard from on a variety of topics. They are likely to express their views directly to the institution on residence hall conditions, campus security, academic advising, the academic calendar, drug and alcohol policies, health services, student behavior, class size, the quality of instruction, and many other topics. CSAOs may choose to ignore this input, or they can merely respond to parents' complaints in a defensive manner; however, if they do this, the confidence parents have in the institution will quickly erode and the students themselves will become antagonistic toward their own university. Also, if the CSAO does not demonstrate care or sensitivity to parents' concerns, they will often turn to the president, the governing board, or the legislature to voice their complaints. Once this process begins, it is very difficult to stop it, and the reputation of the college may be damaged as a result. Parents talk with their children and with other members of their local communities, of course, and if they frequently express negative views about the campus, it may affect admissions and for that matter the credibility of the institution itself. Most presidents expect the CSAO to assume the major responsibility for working with parents. How should the student affairs leader do this?

Listen to Parent Concerns. Chief student affairs administrators, especially those who are new in their positions, should approach parent relations with an open mind. Preconceived notions about parents' attitudes toward the college can lead to unwise decisions and poorly planned programs. Student affairs leaders should listen to others on the campus about parent relations, but they should be prepared to make their own independent assessments of how parents perceive the college. This can be done in several ways, but CSAOs should be direct participants in the process themselves. Information gathered from written questionnaires and randomly placed telephone calls can be very helpful, though it is usually not as valuable as face-to-face discussions with parents. The CSAO can arrange a series of meetings in a variety of locations with parent groups, and the reactions and views gained from such contacts can play a role in developing good parent relations. Many CSAOs have found that the mere gesture of inviting parents to participate in such discussions is genuinely appreciated, and sends an important message that someone at the college cares about them. Of course, if such meetings are not followed up with actions, then it is probable that parent confidence in the institution will diminish, making any later conciliatory efforts very difficult.

Be Sensitive to Parent Feedback. Once the CSAO has opened the door to parent participation and involvement, it is very likely that they will express strong views on a number of campus issues, including some in areas not under the general administrative purview of student affairs. This, of course, can become a source of some irritation to some administrators and faculty on the campus, who did not ask for parent feedback and may not appreciate hearing what they consider to be uninformed opinions about their programs. If CSAOs have essentially acted alone in initiating parent contacts, without involving other key administrators and faculty in the process, they probably deserve the wrath they will inevitably incur. Moreover, a great deal of effort will be required to recover from such a mistake, and to earn back the confidence of colleagues. CSAOs should know in advance that information gained from parents can be quite threatening to some campus officials. It should not be avoided just because it may be unsettling, but it can be approached positively with an institutionwide commitment, shared by key administrators and faculty. The CSAO is the point person for the campus in parent relations, and should persuade the institutional management team that the effort is important in improving campus services and programs. This requires thoughtful planning and the presentation of a workable design for effective parent involvement that is appropriate to the college.

Build Campus Support. Depending on the special needs of the campus, the CSAO may propose an elected parents' advisory council, a campuswide parents' weekend program, a parents' association, a monthly newsletter, a parents' handbook, a series of issue-oriented advisory groups, and a regular parent assessment program. Regardless of the approach taken, conducting a successful campuswide parents' program requires considerable planning, organization, personnel, and fiscal resources. The CSAO is the person who should initiate and orchestrate the process, but another student affairs staff member will probably conduct the actual program. The primary task of the CSAO is to convince members of the management team that the program is necessary and that it deserves support from all areas of the campus. But before any proposals are discussed with the college's management team, the CSAO should meet with key student organization leaders, influential faculty and administrators, and student affairs staff to secure their support and involvement.

Seek Financial Support. If the institution is genuine in its efforts to reach out to parents, seeking their involvement and participation, they will probably be grateful. Among the most effective ways for CSAOs to benefit from parent participation is to share a current campus problem with them and inform them of some of the alternatives being considered as responses to it. If there is a parents' advisory council, this approach gives that group something of substance to address, with the expectation to contribute to the solution. In the process, financial support often is volunteered when parents understand a need. They may become a potential source of support for special programs or projects that cannot be funded from regular college funds. And of course parents can provide insights into student experiences that are not available from anyone else.

Respond to Parent Expectations. The life of the CSAO is seldom calm and noncontroversial, and parents inevitably will be concerned with such volatile issues as security, drug and alcohol abuse, and racial relations. What if parents demand a level of personal security in the residence halls that is completely out of touch with the ways students live in the 1990s? What if parents desire a level of medical and psychological support the institution simply cannot afford? What if some parents are intolerant of the institution's efforts to recruit minority students and to provide special support services to them? Some CSAOs may feel they are already overloaded with too much advice on such matters, without adding yet another dimension — parents! But to ignore the views of parents on these issues is a mistake that can cost the college heavily in terms of understanding and support. Even though there will rarely be unanimous agreement in a parents' council on these controversial issues, a series of frank and honest discussions with them will certainly result in better understanding and support. CSAOs and their staff have an educational role to play with parents as well as with students. Over a period of time, the college can build very solid relations with parents, and both parents and the institution can learn to live with some of the inevitable disagreements that will occur. The most important aspect of the effort must be to express a genuine and honest concern for parent involvement. It is the responsibility of the CSAO to initiate contact with parents, persuade others it is worthwhile, and see to it that it is implemented successfully.

The Governing Board

The primary responsibility for working with the governing board rests, of course, with the president. However, CSAOs also have extensive contact with the board and should work to assure that their concerns are effectively represented in board discussions and decisions. They should attend all meetings of the board, and should know each member well. The backgrounds and educational priorities of board members differ, and student affairs leaders need to understand these differences clearly as they work with their campus presidents in building support for policies, programs, and facilities.

Establish a Student Life Committee. Most governing boards have regular standing committees, and if a committee on student life does not already exist, the CSAO should work with the president to establish one. The student affairs leader should know members of the board well enough to suggest specific names to serve on the committee, and should have talked with board members in advance about what such a committee would do and what it could accomplish for the institution. The CSAO should have prepared a proposal for the president that describes the role of the committee, its suggested composition, and its reason for being. This committee can provide an effective forum for the consideration of policies, programs, resources, and facilities for all areas under the jurisdiction of the student affairs division. It can give high visibility to student life issues on a regular basis, and it can result in substantial improvements in student affairs through the recommendations it makes to the board as a whole. Of course, governing board committees on student life can also become barriers for positive things the CSAO wants to accomplish, if the members of the committee are not well informed or if their priorities clash with those of the president and the CSAO. This is why it is so important for the student affairs leader to develop good relations and support with members of this committee, to educate them about campus issues, and to earn their trust and confidence.

Involve Board Members in Campus Life. CSAOs must always take their direction in board relations from their presidents, but once they have their president's approval, they should find ways to involve key board members in student-related events and programs. A frequent problem for board members is that they may only visit the campus three or four times per year, and may not be attuned to the changes that have taken place in student life since they were in college. How can they make good policies and decide educational priorities if they have not been in a residence hall or a sorority house, have not seen students discussing various issues at a student government meeting, have not listened directly to the concerns of minority students, or have not become familiar with the critical importance of financial aid? The CSAO should provide these experiences to selected board members, not just to assist them in their responsibilities but to increase the likelihood that they will make wise decisions and policies. Selecting the right board members to participate in campus events that can best inform them about important issues requires a good deal of planning on the part of the CSAO. It also requires that the CSAO have a very strong and open relationship with students. If students trust and respect the CSAO, they are more likely to cooperate with plans to inform board members in positive ways. If they do not like the CSAO, they may use their contacts with board members to embarrass the student affairs leader, to criticize programs and policies in student life, or even to urge his or her removal.

Build Board-Student Relations. On topics such as tuition increases, admissions requirements, minority recruiting, athletics, or investment policies, students on most campuses will express themselves to the board, even if there is no established seat on the board for a student or if there is no committee on student life. It is the responsibility of the CSAO, working with the president, to develop effective and orderly ways that student voices can be heard by the board. It is, of course, the board's decision as to how it will choose to involve students in its business, but the student affairs leader should be very active in suggesting ways this can be done. No one else should have better information about student issues and student politics than the CSAO; moreover, presidents expect them to handle such matters.

Provide Information. Most of the issues CSAOs address with their governing boards are not confrontational in nature, but involve the review of policies or the presentation of proposals on needed facilities or programs on the campus. This, of course, requires that the student affairs leader provide excellent reports and information to the board about various issues. Most experienced CSAOs have developed personal and informal contacts with various board members, and often test out their ideas for major policy changes well in advance of formal consideration by the board. Again, the CSAO must be certain that the president is fully in accord with any such informal contacts with board members. More than one CSAO has been dismissed because contacts were made with board members on sensitive issues without the president's knowledge or approval.

Communicate Effectively. Student affairs leaders may be very effective in gaining support for new programs and services with students, faculty, and the community, but if they do not develop good relations with the governing board, they may find their efforts ending up with a negative vote by the board. There are no substitutes for competency and integrity for CSAOs in their relations with the board; those who try to play petty politics will be quickly exposed and viewed with disdain. Most governing board members are highly successful and sophisticated leaders in their own professions, and will respond positively to sensitive and thoughtful proposals that will improve the quality of student life. CSAOs should understand that it is necessary for them to communicate effectively with governing board members in order to accomplish their goals.

The Legislature and the Federal Government

CSAOs have a responsibility to pay close attention to the actions of the state legislature and the federal government, because of the impact of laws passed or considered. This is especially true, of course, for public universities, but it is increasingly pertinent for those in the independent sector as well. Issues such as student financial aid, athletics, health, prepaid tuition programs, minority recruitment and admissions policies, housing loans, disabled student programs, child care, assessment, crime reporting requirements, and student confidentiality laws are critical to the institution, and the CSAO should be the best-informed administrator on the campus regarding them.

Communicate with Key Leaders. At most colleges and universities, there is a staff member assigned specific responsibility for legislative and governmental relations. The CSAO should work closely with this individual, and should become personally acquainted with the members of the local legislative delegations. Presidents, of course, are the institutional spokespersons on all legislative matters, and CSAOs should take their lead from them. However, a great deal can be accomplished by means of personal, informal conversations between legislators and the student affairs leader. If CSAOs take the time to study important legislative issues, and become well informed regarding them, they can become reliable and trusted resource persons for legislators and their staffs. If they have thoughtful suggestions regarding laws or policies under consideration, then it is likely they will be sought out for their views, especially if they demonstrate a genuine interest in the legislation that goes beyond parochial institutional concerns. Many CSAOs have established reputations for their expertise on issues being considered by state legislatures and the Congress, and are called to testify on specific bills. Of course, such participation must always have the support of the campus president. Formal testimony is time consuming, takes the student affairs leader away from the campus, and is not very exciting after it has been done a few times. The informal contacts CSAOs make with members of their local delegations and their staffs are far more important in their impact.

Take the Initiative. Because there are so many bills filed in state legislatures and in Congress every year, it is very easy for CSAOs to feel that their role is mainly defensive and reactive in nature. A great deal of time is required simply to respond in useful ways to all the proposed legislation. But most CSAOs want to do more than just respond to bills written by others; they have strong commitments of their own that they think should be enacted. Considerable effort is necessary to take positive initiatives, such as working with members of the local delegation to introduce new laws and programs that might benefit the institution and its students. The best student affairs leaders find ways to do this, because they feel such involvement is part of their overall leadership responsibility for their institutions. Presidents deserve to have CSAOs who are well informed about legislation in all areas related to student welfare, and who are capable of implementing effective actions.

Keep Students Informed. On most campuses, there are many politically active students who are well informed about legislative matters and who follow them closely. Some have formalized their interests into actual lobbying groups and have become quite influential on such matters as student fees and financial aid. But even (or especially) in the absence of well-organized student efforts, CSAOs have a responsibility to share with student leaders the implications of various proposals being considered by lawmaking bodies. For example, over one-half of the students at a college may be recipients of financial aid, and if a bill is presented in Congress to require drug testing for all aid recipients, it certainly needs to be brought to the attention of students. The student affairs leader should make sure that this is done in a timely and effective manner. Caution must be taken so as not to lead students to a particular point of view on legislative matters, especially at publicly supported institutions. If lawmakers feel that campus administrators are using students as their mouthpieces on controversial issues, they will understandably be very upset. It is an ethical responsibility of the CSAO to inform students about pending legislation and its possible implications, but not to persuade them to adopt a particular point of view.

Support the President. Colleges and universities express their opinions on various issues to their legislative delegations through their presidents. Because there are so many issues, it is inevitable that the CSAO will disagree with the official position of the institution from time to time. For example, a state legislature may be considering a bill that will create a merit scholarship program designed to attract very gifted students. The CSAO may feel strongly that state funds should instead be placed in programs designed to help poor and disadvantaged students. However, the president supports the merit bill, convinced that it will enhance the academic image of the college. This type of conflict is not unusual, and it poses a difficult dilemma for student affairs leaders. Their responsibility is to represent their views as persuasively as they can within their institutions, and then to support the official positions taken by their presidents. Student affairs leaders cannot get into public debate with their presidents or governing board members on legislative issues. Such discussion should occur within the institution, since presidents must present clear, unified messages on legislative matters for them to be effective. If there is such frequent disagreement that the CSAO no longer feels comfortable at the institution, then it is time to move elsewhere. In all of their work with legislation, they should remember that their most important responsibility is to represent the educational and social needs of the students.

Donors and Alumni

Student affairs leaders can enhance opportunities for students by becoming actively involved in fund raising and alumni affairs. Development staff should be well informed about student affairs, and establishing good relations with donors and alumni should result in more support for programs and facilities in student life. Donors and alumni are not just important to private colleges and universities; public institutions are now conducting very intensive efforts to enhance relations with these groups.

Attend Alumni Functions. The student affairs leader should be quite visible to alumni, and this is best done by attending alumni meetings throughout the year and finding opportunities to talk about the various needs in the division. Such activities, of course, must be coordinated with other institutional needs, but alumni can be very helpful in student recruitment, scholarship support, employment internships, and many other areas. They can also be a valuable resource as advisers on difficult or controversial campus issues, and CSAOs should seek effective ways to call on them. The best alumni may lose interest in their alma mater if they are only asked to give money; most are genuinely concerned about policies, programs, and facilities, and will appreciate invitations to express their views and offer their suggestions.

Form an Advisory Group. The CSAO may want to consider forming a specific alumni advisory group on student affairs, as a subcommittee of the institutionwide alumni board. This may ensure that student life needs will be regularly represented in the total alumni program, and may also provide the CSAO with a valuable sounding board on campus issues and problems. This has been done successfully at Lehigh University, where the CSAO has established a Visiting Team of Alumni to review and improve student life programs and policies. Because of the varied interests of alumni, the CSAO may want to encourage several alumni groups to form, so that such special needs as child care, admissions, student aid, campus recreation, student leadership, minority concerns, and health services can be addressed. This requires a good deal of time as well as effective coordination with the chief development officer. But if student affairs leaders can find the time to develop good alumni relations, the effort can pay handsome dividends for program support and facilities.

Get Active with Potential Donors. Donors can be alumni or friends of the institution. Colleges and universities, both private and public, have become very aggressive in fund-raising programs in recent years, and CSAOs should be active participants. They cannot spend a great deal of their time on fund raising, but they cannot ignore this important responsibility. They should try to identify potential donors for specific programs and facilities, not depending entirely on professional fund raisers, whose primary activity may be in other areas. With the support of the chief development officer, they can seek meetings with potential donors, and often these contacts can lead to support that cannot be realized in any other way.

Inform Donors and Alumni About Student Life. CSAOs have a special responsibility to keep donors and alumni well informed about the changing nature of student life. They should make sure that articles appear in the alumni magazine on student life issues and programs. Such information can go a long way in advancing understanding and support for student affairs. But this support will only be helpful if it is based on an understanding of current problems and needs, not ones that may have existed decades ago.

Support Ethical Standards. Student affairs leaders rarely have enough financial resources to do all the things they would like to do for students. Working with donors and alumni offers the best opportunity available to them to find additional sources of support. But because there are so many needs, it may be tempting to accept support from donors and alumni without paying careful attention to ethical principles. Is the money being donated coming from a source that the institution can support? Do the donors or alumni expect that their gift will give them special consideration in admissions or residence hall assignments? Will receipt of a gift place the college in an untenable position with certain ethnic or minority groups? While CSAOs are not the primary decision makers regarding campus fund raising, they are part of the management team, and they must raise questions about student-related matters that might present ethical problems or conflicts of interest for the institution.

If student affairs leaders feel that these problems or conflicts are unacceptable, then they have a responsibility to discuss them directly with their presidents and to come to an acceptable resolution.

The Student Affairs Staff

One of the most important tasks of the CSAO is to develop a highly committed, loyal, and professionally oriented staff. Very little can be accomplished without this group's support, and the success of the student affairs leader depends on the way the staff performs and the way it is perceived.

Earn Their Support. Because student affairs has grown and has become so diverse, the chief administrator must learn to work effectively with medical doctors, police chiefs, child-care directors, counseling psychologists, athletic directors, housing officers, financial aid specialists, and religious advisers. CSAOs must earn the support and respect of their staff every day. This is not necessarily easy, because all staff members have had professional training specific to their positions, and all assume they should function according to relatively autonomous standards. The student affairs leader, especially one new to the campus, may also be viewed by some staff members as a politician-bureaucrat, not as a professional educator. This may be particularly true if the new CSAO has not come up through the ranks. How, then, does the student affairs leader build strong support from the staff, and earn their respect and loyalty?

Demonstrate Competence. To be successful with their own staff, CSAOs must demonstrate professional competence, a willingness to work hard, personal integrity, and an ability to listen. A failure to perform well in any of these areas may result in the eventual dismissal or resignation of the student affairs leader. Professional competence is necessary to lead the staff on issues, problems, and policies.

Understand Higher Education. Student affairs leaders will not convince their staff of their professional competence by being elected to national offices or by giving clever speeches; they will earn the confidence of their staff by their day-to-day performance on the job, showing by their actions that they are in tune with the needs of the students. They must find the time to educate themselves about each of the professional areas within the student affairs division for which they are responsible. They cannot do a good job of leading the health service, the police department, the counseling center, or the financial aid office if they are not familiar with the professional journals in each area, understand the professional issues being faced by the staff, and attend some of their meetings and conferences. If the staff members in any of these departments feel that the CSAO is not well informed about their field, they will have little respect or time for anything he or she does. More generally, student affairs leaders should have an understanding of American higher education, so that current problems and future possibilities can be put in a developmental perspective; a research-based knowledge of students, their characteristics, and how they learn and grow; of social organizations and how they can be changed; of educational philosophy and social psychology; of management and financial standards; and of the social, legal, political, and ethical issues that shape the modern university. All this requires continued learning, and CSAOs should demonstrate their commitment to vigorous lifelong professional development. In short, there are many experienced professionals working in student affairs in the 1990s, and those who lead them must have a high level of competence to earn the confidence and support of these staff members.

Accept the Time Demands of the Job. Being a CSAO requires hard work and long hours. It is not a position for someone seeking an orderly, predictable, and calm way of life! The issues faced, the student activity, the diversity of programs, and the demands of other people all add up to an extremely challenging schedule. In the interviews conducted as part of this study, most CSAOs reported that they spent between sixty and seventy hours per week doing their jobs. Most saw no substitute for doing this, and most also mentioned that many of their staff members worked similar schedules.

It is difficult for student affairs leaders to win the respect and support of their staff if they are not seen as working hard. This does not require martyrdom or a workaholic schedule; it simply means that staff members should know that their leader is strongly committed to what needs to be done and is willing to do what is necessary to get there. If this can be pursued with zest, not with drudgery, then the staff is likely to develop positive attitudes as well. Long hours for student affairs staff, however, should be addressed by the CSAO with the staff, because too many talented people have left the profession because of this problem. Ways need to be found to help professional staff in student affairs work smarter, not longer.

Be a Mentor and Teacher. A very important responsibility of the CSAO is to encourage professional growth and development on the part of staff members, especially those relatively new to the profession. Expressing a personal interest in the career of a young assistant director in admissions, a residence hall adviser, or a newly appointed police officer often results in positive outcomes. Providing funds for such staff to attend conferences or enroll in graduate courses can also be helpful. Some young student affairs staff members may lack confidence to initiate a new program, and may benefit from having a mentor-type relationship with the CSAO. Student affairs staff who have been in middle-management positions for several years may also appreciate personal contacts with the CSAO regarding their career and professional plans. Assuming a mentor or teaching role with the student affairs staff does not require the CSAO to be an expert on everything. The important message to convey is a genuine concern for the current and future status of individual personnel. If this can be done over a period of time and reinforced by real support for staff, the benefits can be considerable. Many experienced CSAOs report that some of their greatest satisfaction comes from seeing younger staff members whom they have nurtured move on to significant and successful assignments.

Demonstrate Integrity. No attribute is more important in earning the support of the student affairs staff than integrity. In all of their relations with the staff, CSAOs must demonstrate honesty: in decisions about evaluation, promotion, and compensation; in support for proposals; in the handling of grievances; in maintaining confidences; and in day-to-day personal contacts. Student affairs leaders must do what they say, and conduct themselves in a professional manner, regardless of the setting. They must demonstrate genuine concern for their staff without showing favoritism toward anyone, and must avoid personal relations with staff members that may compromise their professional effectiveness. The staff do not expect the CSAO to be a saint, but they do expect their leader to stand for sound educational and ethical principles and to act on them. They expect their leader to represent their aspirations and proposals to the president, the students, and all other constituencies with openness and honesty. They also expect to be treated as professionals themselves, being kept informed and involved in genuine efforts to meet the needs of the students.

Listen to Staff Concerns. If there is a universal characteristic of student affairs staff, it is that they all want to be heard. Most experienced CSAOs understand this and know that it is far less important for them to make speeches than to listen to their own staff. This is a difficult lesson for some newly appointed student affairs leaders to learn, since they are often so anxious to get underway with "their program" that they forget to sit down with staff and hear their ideas, concerns, and proposals. Failure to do this usually results in the CSAOs' being perceived by staff as arrogant, distant, uninformed, and insensitive. Listening to staff must be done in a genuine manner, not as a way to manipulate opinions or change. CSAOs must show some patience in this process, because they cannot go much faster with policy change or program development than their staff will allow. Staff members' ideas must be taken seriously and reflected to a considerable extent in subsequent actions.

Not only should student affairs leaders listen to their staff, they should also know them well. Even on large campuses, the best CSAOs know the names of all the staff members, and try to learn and remember important details about each of them.

Getting to know individual staff members and demonstrating a willingness to listen to them can build a positive, professional climate, where ideas and opinions can be shared openly. The best CSAOs work to establish relations with their staff where policies and programs can be considered on their merit, and staff can engage in vigorous debate without losing professional respect for one another. If student affairs leaders become good listeners with their staff, know them well, and respect their judgment, they will have taken very important steps toward earning their support.

One of the most challenging aspects of the CSAO position is that various constituencies frequently have different expectations regarding student life policies and programs. The success of the CSAO is largely dependent on his or her ability to mediate conflicts and disagreements among these groups without losing the support of any of them, while also managing the organization effectively and moving it toward its educational goals. This focus on management, mediation, and education will be the subject of the next three chapters.

Part Two

Administrative Roles and Responsibilities

5

The Manager

Student affairs leaders may establish candid relations with presidents, students, faculty, the community, and other constituencies, but if they do not manage their divisions efficiently, they will be a failure. They are accountable for the programs, policies, facilities, and financial resources of the entire division. CSAOs need to know what they want to accomplish and how they plan to do it. They must have a good understanding of the university as an organization, a sensitivity to the needs of others, sound fiscal skills, and a familiarity with effective management practices. Successful management requires attention to detail, hard work, and thoughtful planning. This chapter discusses the role of the student affairs leader as manager and presents suggestions for effective practice as well.

Developing a Plan

The most important initial requirement for good management of student affairs is to have a plan. CSAOs must have a clear idea of what they want to accomplish. Their plans should reflect a point of view about education that is consistent with their own beliefs and with the purposes of their institutions. If they are not clear about where they want to go with student affairs, it will result in lack of support from the president, confusion for the students, and frustration for the staff. The effective student affairs manager is a leader whose vision and enthusiasm should cause others to support student life. How does the CSAO go about developing a good plan for effective management?

Know the Institution. There is no philosophical orthodoxy, and no universal management prescription that fits all campuses, in student affairs. A major mistake made by student affairs leaders is to duplicate what they have done at a previous college in their new institution. The plan must reflect the distinctive character of the college, the composition and abilities of the student body, the community setting, the available resources, and the sophistication of the student affairs staff. The CSAO must make careful and realistic assessments of these factors in order to develop a workable plan. Common pitfalls for student affairs managers are to overestimate their potential resources and to misjudge the actual interests and priorities of their students. Such errors result in frustration, since the plans do not fit the institution and so are not embraced by students or others.

Make the Plan Credible. A good plan for effective management of student affairs should include a credible rationale, one that is consistent with the purposes of the institution and is understandable to all members of the university community. It should include the outcomes the CSAO wants to achieve with students, stated in reasonable and convincing language; it should include a clear presentation of the major programs, policies, and facilities needed; and it should include a description of an organizational structure to carry out the plan. The CSAO has the responsibility for developing this plan and for implementing it successfully. However, such a plan cannot be developed in isolation by the student affairs leader and simply imposed on students, faculty, and staff. Organizations consist of people, and they function most efficiently when the members have a real stake in deciding and carrying out their goals. This is especially true in student affairs, where there are so many groups that feel they should have a role in deciding policy. By collaborating with faculty, students, and others, the CSAO can build support and greatly increase the chances of success. A given, of course, is that what the student affairs manager wants to accomplish must have the understanding and support of the president before it is pursued.

Move Ahead with the Plan. A difficult problem for CSAOs is that they rarely have adequate time to develop their plans. When they assume their positions, there are high expectations for them to make changes and improvements quickly, or to solve problems that have been left unattended by years. In many cases, they have been hired to correct some management or leadership deficiencies that existed previously. There may be immediate needs that need addressing, such as low enrollment, inefficiency in delivering financial aid, or an absence of child care. It is not unusual for CSAOs to be contacted several weeks prior to their actual appointments by campus and community groups that are demanding a new service, policy, or program. Within such settings, student affairs leaders do not have the luxury of spending a year on the development of a plan! They are expected to deliver successful programs right away by their presidents, by the students, and by others. Moreover, any plan must be developed concurrent with the day-by-day problems of managing the division. This requires aggressive, strong leaders who can effectively present a plan, involve others, win their support, and move forward without delay. Many CSAOs have had the initiative taken away from them, because they have moved too slowly or have not been forceful enough with their plans. When this happens there is confusion about who is really in charge and about how change will occur. It is also very difficult for CSAOs who have lost their initiative to regain it. Others may perceive them as passive and vulnerable and not very influential in getting things done. This is not to suggest a defensive approach to the management of student affairs. It does mean, however, that CSAOs must assume the leadership for the division as soon as they arrive, developing a plan of action in a timely manner and implementing it aggressively. In the absence of strong leadership by the CSAO, other less effective mechanisms will emerge from other areas of the campus to address student needs. In other cases, these needs will simply not be addressed at all.

Share the Plan with Others. A plan for good management, of course, does not implement itself. It must be shared with others, supported by the president, and pushed by the CSAO. The first of these points requires emphasis. Some newly appointed student affairs leaders may be disappointed when their operational plans are not met with wild enthusiasm by others on the campus; they must learn that faculty, other administrators, and students all have their own agendas, and that it requires considerable effort just to get their attention, not to mention their support. Moreover, the various constituencies on and off campus are mostly interested in results, not plans. CSAOs will be judged on the basis of their ability to manage programs and deliver services, not on the beauty of their elaborate plans. The primary benefit of a good management plan is to guide student affairs leaders in their efforts to implement their objectives. While the plan may not be overly exciting to others, it is mandatory for the effective management of the student affairs division — and it must be shared with others on campus in a timely fashion.

Strategies for Implementing the Plan

A variety of approaches can be taken by CSAOs in implementing their management plans. Colleges and universities differ greatly in their composition and purposes, and student affairs leaders must adjust their strategies to fit the particular needs of their institution. Moreover, the educational backgrounds of CSAOs are diverse, and the special emphases they give to their work can vary. Regardless of the campus, or the priorities of the student affairs leader, there are a number of issues that must be addressed as the management plan is implemented. Among these are the administrative structure and reporting lines, centralization versus decentralization in decision making, the involvement of various groups in the division's affairs, and the allocation of resources.

Administrative Structure and Reporting Lines. Effective student affairs managers will want organizations that encourage open communication among departments, enable students and faculty to participate in them, and keep the CSAO well informed about issues and problems. In deciding the organizational arrangement, CSAOs should understand that how far they distance themselves from staff and students may send out an important message. If the student affairs leader appears to be accessible only in a remote way, because of a multilayered organizational chart, there may be negative perceptions that can hinder program effectiveness. On the other hand, if the CSAO wants to please everyone by being accessible at all times to anyone who asks, then staff members may become frustrated and confused regarding their own roles. Both approaches affect the way the student affairs leader is viewed on the campus.

The organization of the division should be clear and understandable to those outside student affairs as well as to the staff itself. Reporting lines should be unambiguous and should reflect real responsibility and authority. The CSAO must make sure the organization functions in a way that accurately reflects the formal, written chart. This chart should not be a rigid document that restricts the movement or communication of staff, but it must serve as an agreed-on map of how things will get done. At most colleges and universities, student affairs divisions have become so diverse that many of the departments are physically dispersed around the campus. Moreover, it may be difficult for some staff members to see a logical connection among such areas as child care, admissions, security, and intercollegiate athletics. This makes it all the more important for the CSAO to develop an organizational arrangement that is clear and easily understood. If the staff realizes that the way things really get done has no relationship to the organizational chart, then there will be confusion and cynicism.

The organizational chart is not just an inert piece of paper used once per year in an annual report. It should be an accurate description of how the CSAO wants the division to operate, a dynamic instrument that changes as the needs of the campus dictate. Such changes need to be made with caution, though. Reorganization within a student affairs division is sometimes used as a way to "solve" personnel problems, or program issues that the CSAO does not want to confront directly. But such action is almost always a mistake, because these problems are rarely, if ever, solved by simply changing the organizational chart. A sweeping organizational change can be very traumatic for staff, especially if it is carried out by a CSAO who has not consulted widely with those affected.

Centralization Versus Decentralization. Finding the right balance between a centralized and a decentralized organization is a very important task for the CSAO in managing the division. Going too far in either direction may have negative consequences in quality of programs, consistency of policies, and the morale of staff. It may also affect the reputation and effectiveness of the CSAO as a manager, since he or she will be held accountable for whatever happens in the division. The particular organizational model will vary with the size and complexity of the institution and with the preferred style of the student affairs leader. On smaller campuses, it may be natural for the CSAO to assume the central role in decision making, since there may be only fifteen or twenty professional staff members in the entire division, and personal contacts among all of them may occur each day. At large universities, by contrast, there may be hundreds of staff members in the division, and the CSAO's contacts may be primarily with the several department heads. In this case, a decentralized approach is often more logical. However, in all cases, the criterion for deciding which approach to take should be the effective delivery of programs and services to students.

A newly appointed student affairs manager may be concerned that there has been too much autonomy in the decisions made by the various departments, and that this has resulted in confusion for the students, inconsistent quality of programs, and anger on the part of the president. In an effort to correct these serious problems, the CSAO may decide to centralize all important programmatic and policy decisions in his or her office. This may ensure that certain mistakes will be avoided and will send a strong message to the staff and to others as to who is in charge. However, it may have a very negative impact on staff morale and on their willingness to initiate new programs and ideas. It may also seriously damage the professional relationship between the CSAO and the rest of the staff, since they may believe their leader has no confidence in them.

Excellent communication and a highly professional staff are essential, however, for a decentralized management plan to work well in student affairs. The CSAO must establish clear expectations for staff members and have confidence in their ability to manage on the basis of trust. Even in the best of circumstances, it is inevitable in a strongly decentralized division that some actions will be taken by the staff that will surprise the CSAO, expose some inconsistency in procedures, or challenge some institutionwide policy. Student affairs leaders usually find themselves explaining such shortcomings to their presidents, to other administrative colleagues, and to confused or amused students. Most experienced CSAOs realize that they have to live with the inevitable problems associated with decentralization if they are going to attract and retain strong staff. But they also understand that if there are too many inconsistencies and embarrassments caused by overeager personnel acting on their own, they will lose support from the president, and others, who will view the student affairs leader as a poor manager.

Involvement of Others in Decisions. The student affairs leader must have a clear idea of how the division should be organized, and needs to find an approach that works well regarding the centralization-decentralization issue. An equally important management task is to decide how to involve various groups in the decision-making process and in the setting of priorities for the division. Student affairs programs cannot succeed if they are isolated from the mainstream of the campus, and function best when many groups have a role in deciding what happens. The best CSAOs understand that it is their responsibility to devise effective ways of involving these groups in policy and program decisions. This is a critical function that must be managed skillfully in order to achieve positive results.

Student affairs leaders should not invite groups to participate in the process of deciding programs and policies if they themselves are unsure of what the desired outcomes are, however. As the managers responsible for their division, they should have clear notions of where they want to go, and should be able to provide strong direction to others. Faculty and student groups invited to participate in formulating student affairs policies and programs expect strong guidance from the CSAO, and should never simply be handed a blank check to pursue whatever whims they may have. Moreover, if they are not given clear direction, they will most likely view the CSAO as passive and vulnerable, and will not respect this administrator's management skills. This is not to suggest that the effective CSAO is a political bully, or that involvement of others is just a manipulative tool to gain support or to co-opt others. Student affairs leaders cannot manage their divisions by fiat, nor can they simply delegate all authority to others. The decision to involve others must be genuine, reflecting a sincere desire to solicit ideas and suggestions. But students, faculty, and other groups should understand that their role is advisory, and that the final decision-making responsibility remains with the CSAO and the president.

The following example illustrates how CSAOs can involve others in the decision-making process. At a public, medium-size university, students, faculty, community members, parents, and alumni have all expressed concern about unruly student behavior at athletic events, at weekend parties on campus, and in campus residences. While all groups are not demanding the same actions, it is clear to the newly appointed CSAO that significant changes in the student conduct code and the judicial system are necessary. But even though the student affairs leader has had extensive experience in implementing student conduct programs in previous positions on other campuses, she knows she cannot simply install a new policy without extensive involvement and discussion with all of these groups. She convinces the president to appoint a task force composed of influential members of the various groups (after personally consulting with each of them), and gives the task force a specific charge and target date for their work. She makes sure that a very experienced and trusted faculty member serves as chair, and asks a knowledgeable and respected student affairs staff member to assist the task force in its work. She urges the members to invite outside experts to advise it, and provides the task force with adequate financial and information resources to accomplish its objectives. Most importantly, she meets personally with the group, explaining clearly to them what she is asking them to do and assuring them that she will give their recommendations careful consideration in her final decision about a new student conduct system. She presents some alternative models to the committee and shares her own educational goals for the program with them. Thus, the CSAO has a clear idea of where she wants to go with the student conduct program, but recognizes the necessity of involving concerned groups in the decision-making process. There are risks in this approach, of course, because the resulting recommendations may not be exactly what the CSAO had hoped for. However, by taking the aggressive and open steps just described, she stands a very good chance of getting a workable new policy. Just as important, she will have a policy that all concerned groups had a genuine role in deciding.

This can be a slow and often frustrating process for the CSAO, since further student conduct problems are most likely occurring while the task force is doing its work. Since such problems get a lot of attention, the CSAO will be under a good deal of pressure from the president, the other vice presidents, and others to solve the matter quickly without waiting for a committee to finally make its recommendations. It is the responsibility of the student affairs leader to explain her strategy in advance to these people, convincing them that the process is necessary to achieve the desired results and that there will be some unpleasantness before it is done. Of course, the CSAO also knows that the final result must work and must produce real improvements, or her credibility as a manager will be seriously compromised. This process may be repeated on other issues and problems, and the same carefully planned methods of involving others need to be followed by the student affairs leader.

Most CSAOs establish standing advisory groups on a wide variety of programs and policies, feeling that continuity will result in positive outcomes. Thus, advisory groups on child care, admissions, campus security, and financial aid can be formed, and over a period of time can develop into very helpful groups. However, simply having them in place does not automatically result in good advice and evaluation. The student affairs leader must nurture these groups, providing them with extensive information, discussing important issues with them, and thanking them for their contribution. Even though there may be several such advisory groups, the CSAO must find the time to

work with all of them. Each campus has its own method of appointing faculty and students to these committees, and the student affairs leader should take an active role in this process, to
ensure that those appointed are qualified and committed to their
task. Of course, if the CSAO selects the people to serve on the
various advisory boards, the process will be very suspect, especially among students. CSAOs should use their influence with
the faculty senate and with the student government to ensure
that the roles and functions of the committees are understood,
that those who serve have an important responsibility, and that
those appointed are representative of the diversity of the campus.
It is especially important to work closely with the chairs of each
of the advisory committees, establishing rapport and understanding, so that the most effective leadership can be exerted. The
CSAO should also see that special efforts are made to educate
student members of the advisory groups, since their membership
usually changes each year. This can be done in cooperative
efforts with the committee chairs, or with all students who are
selected to serve. The student affairs leader has an ethical responsibility to consider seriously and honestly the advice these groups
provide. Students and faculty are being asked to volunteer their
time and effort to improve services for students, and the CSAO
has an obligation to make their involvement worthwhile. The
credibility of student affairs officers will be seriously damaged
if they ignore these advisory groups, do not take them seriously,
or treat them in a patronizing manner. Inviting students, faculty,
and others to participate in the decision-making process is serious business, and it is the duty of the CSAO to see that it is
done in a vigorous and genuine manner.

Allocation of Resources. The student affairs administrator needs
to decide how to allocate the available financial resources as part
of the overall management strategy. As part of this effort, the
CSAO must also determine ways of securing the resources
needed to accomplish the division's objectives. These are critically important tasks, and they can have a major impact on the
success of the student affairs leader. In many ways, the student
affairs staff may evaluate the effectiveness of CSAOs in direct

proportion to their ability to provide the necessary resources to meet the needs of their department. Staff, programs, and facilities cost money, and CSAOs must work hard to secure the financial resources needed to support them.

The key person for the student affairs leader to convince regarding the needed resources of course is the president. However, before a budgetary request is presented, the CSAO must be sure that it is consistent with the educational objectives of the institution, that it is supported by staff and students, and that all available sources of support have been explored.

Proposals for financial support and the use of these resources must be directed at the most critical needs of the institution and must be consistent with its educational philosophy, as well. If the CSAO is viewed as not investing money and effort in the areas most needing attention, very little support will be gained, and the other administrators will become skeptical about the CSAO's management skills. If the college is attracting insufficient numbers of applicants and has too many students dropping out, it will seem very strange if the CSAO does not propose a major recruitment and retention strategy as part of his or her budgetary request.

Many CSAOs have experienced frustration and failure with their requests for financial support because they attempted to impose their own agendas and priorities on their institutions. They have done this because they misunderstood what the college's real needs were, or because they lacked insight regarding others' views of their plans. This does not mean the student affairs leader has to blindly follow the current mandates of others in the institution in attempts to secure resources. In fact, imaginative student affairs managers may challenge their colleges to alter their plans and policies. For example, the institution may have placed its student aid resources in programs to attract outstanding freshmen for several years, and the CSAO may argue that half of these funds should be used to recruit community college transfers. But student affairs leaders must realize that proposals that deviate too far from the educational priorities of the college will not only fail to win support, but may also damage their reputation as good managers.

Requests for financial support rarely succeed if they are presented without the knowledge and backing of others. Most CSAOs have established advisory councils on a variety of issues and programs, and understand that the faculty, students, parents, and community leaders serving on them can be very helpful in building support for financial resources. They also understand that if they were to seek financial support for a new program or facility without consulting with these groups, they would lose their credibility as managers, and would probably create a good deal of antagonism in the process. For example, if a CSAO is convinced that a new recreation sports facility is badly needed, and proposes this to the president without having consulted with student groups, faculty, and other administrators, the proposal will probably fail, and the groups that were ignored in the process will lose trust and confidence in the student affairs leader. Moreover, such shoddy management may embarrass the president, who may support the new facility, but in speaking with students, discovers that they have not been consulted. Presidents should only be asked for financial resources when student affairs leaders have assured themselves that the important groups have been informed about and support the proposal. The student affairs staff itself also deserves to be involved in budgetary matters, and their support should never be taken for granted by the student affairs leader. Ignoring them may result in very difficult morale problems within the division as well as in a lack of trust in the CSAO as a manager. There are some circumstances, of course, where proposals for financial support may need to go forward without the unanimous consent of all campus groups. For example, the need for a new residence hall may be supported by students, parents, and other administrators, but community leaders and faculty may be opposed to the idea. In such cases, it is the responsibility of the CSAO to assess the feasibility of the project and decide if its benefits outweigh the potential problems it will cause. These should be discussed with other members of the management team, and the president should be fully apprised of the issue before any final decision is made.

A more difficult dilemma for the CSAO occurs when a proposal for financial resources has the backing of student, faculty, and community groups, but is not supported by the other vice presidents of the institution. There is so much competiton for resources, and so many good ideas within most colleges and universities, that this situation is not unusual. The student affairs leader may be convinced that money is needed to fund speakers, seminars, lectures, and new staff to improve racial relations on the campus, but the chief academic officer and the other vice presidents may feel there are more important priorities and that such a volatile issue would be better left alone. Some student affairs leaders may, in their passionate impatience, go directly to the president for support, but they must realize that in doing so, they almost always pay a price with their administrative colleagues. There is a delicate balance of power within the management team of any institution, and the CSAO must be perceptive enough to know when and how to challenge the usual ways of seeking financial support. The most naive student affairs leaders have asked student groups to lobby for them, or have tried "end runs" by seeking support from friends on the governing board. Such efforts are not only unethical in practice; they will infuriate presidents and usually result in the justified termination of the CSAO! Effective student affairs managers who are skillful in involving various groups in proposals for financial support understand the process for securing the resources, and are willing and honest participants in the vigorous competition with their administrative colleagues. They are grateful for the successes they have achieved, and understanding on the occasions when resources are directed to other priorities.

It is the responsibility of the CSAO to explore all possible sources of support for projects and programs. If student affairs leaders rely solely on their president to provide all the needed resources, they will be viewed as passive and unimaginative managers. Moreover, the programs within their divisions will suffer, because very few institutions have adequate money to support all the needed programs and facilities. This is not to suggest that the CSAO must become a full-time fund raiser, or an institutional "scrounger" for money. But presidents are much more likely to provide financial support for proposals if CSAOs can demonstrate that they have already secured half the needed dollars through creative efforts of their own. By working with the development office, other vice presidents, student, community, and parent groups, and state and federal agencies, they can secure significant additional resources for student affairs. The necessity for child care is an example: The CSAO knows that the program will cost $600,000, a figure completely out of the question in terms of direct cash support from the president. However, by creating a small student fee as part of tuition, assessing parent users a monthly charge, securing a federal grant under Title XX, using student interns from the child education department, and converting part of any existing campus building for use, the actual request for funds to the president is only $75,000 annually. Such proposals are likely to be funded because they give evidence of widespread support and solid efforts at self-help. Most important, they demonstrate good management by student affairs leaders who understand the most effective ways to gain financial support for their programs. Presidents will understandably become irritated with CSAOs who have not aggressively explored all the alternatives for the funding of programs and projects. They expect and deserve student affairs leaders who can find ways to augment institutional resources with other funds.

Management Cases

The effective student affairs leader knows the institution well, has developed a plan for achieving realistic objectives, and has formed a strategy for implementing the management plan. This plan has included careful attention to organizational structure, the decision-making process and those who should be involved in it, and the securing and allocation of resources. In this section, three short case studies are presented that illustrate how successful student affairs managers approach and solve actual problems in their divisions.

The Appointment of a New President. At this college, the CSAO worked very successfully for seven years for a president who recruited and hired her, and then the president left the institution. A new president is appointed from outside the college, and is given a mandate by the board to improve graduate education, research, and private fund raising. The previous president was well known to undergraduates, was personally engaged in efforts to improve general education, and encouraged student participation in college policies and programs. But the new chief executive indicates that he will spend most of his time in activities external to the institution and that he expects the CSAO to "take care of all student matters." The student affairs staff is well aware of this shift in priorities and is very apprehensive about it. Student leaders have also discussed the matter with the CSAO and have expressed concern about their role within the college. The student affairs leader is perplexed by the change herself, but she does not want to appear unsure of herself with staff and students. Moreover, she understands her responsibilities to the institution, and as a professional, accepts her obligation to assist the new president in his important transition to the position. As a good manager, what should she do?

The CSAO needs to have a very candid discussion with the new president, preferably before he formally begins the job. It is vastly preferable to have this frank conversation when the president is appointed than it is to face embarrassing and unproductive conflicts several months later. And the CSAO must be forthright in this discussion, even though it may be uncomfortable. She realizes she serves at the pleasure of the president, and if the ideological and managerial fit is not good, then she should resign. The first obligation she has as a professional is to herself: Is the change in educational priorities consistent with her personal goals and objectives? If she is going to have to spend a lot of her time doing things she does not believe are important, she will not be happy and will not be very productive.

Since there is seldom a perfect match between a president and a CSAO, a compromise is often appropriate. The key is to have a clear understanding of what is expected and what support will be provided. In the present example, the student affairs leader may decide she can reach her goals because she is convinced the president will provide her with moral support and financial resources. She realizes that he will not be an active participant in campus life and that she will have to become even more visible in her own management style as a result. She will not have a collegial relationship with the president, since he will be away from the campus most of the time and has more pressing priorities than students. She regrets not having a president she can discuss ideas and problems with on a daily basis, and knows that as a result, she will be much more on her own in the decisions she makes. She is close to her vice presidential colleagues, and knows that each of them will have to make significant adjustments to the new president as well. This can result in the management team's becoming closer and less competitive among themselves, since they will be more dependent on each other than on the president.

Once the CSAO and the president have decided they can work together effectively, the student affairs leader must begin the process of "marketing" the president to the staff and students. She must be supportive of the president and persuasive about his plans to improve the institution. Her actions will affect the way the president is perceived and accepted by staff and students in his first few months. She must be honest with those she serves, of course, and she knows she will have to become a strong advocate with the new president if staff and students are to maintain their current involvement and activity. She will have to be a more forceful and active manager as a result.

A Budget Deficit. In the middle of the fiscal year, the governor announces that severe revenue shortfalls have occurred and that all public agencies and state universities will have to reduce their budgets by 8 percent. The institution is given only three weeks to submit its plan. The president calls the vice presidents to a meeting, and directs them to submit plans to meet this deficit in each of their divisions. They are informed that they have one week to complete this task, and then the president and the vice presidents will decide as a team if some areas will be cut more than others. Because the required cut is substantial and because some 70 percent of the total college budget is in staff salaries, employees will have to be laid off. Since this is such a sensitive problem that could result in legal challenges by staff as well as low morale, the president has directed the vice presidents not to discuss this budget deficit with any staff except the departmental deans and directors. The governor's announcement, of course, was public, and has already caused anxiety among the staff. Only three days after the announcement, the student government association presents the president with a petition, demanding that tuition not be raised, that financial aid not be cut, and that all support services for students be continued. This is a very unpleasant problem for the CSAO to face, and is a severe test of the management skill of this administrator. What should the student affairs leader do?

The good manager has paid close attention to the state budget process and has anticipated this problem. Despite the volatile nature of the issue, the student affairs leader had prepared the department heads two months earlier and had them develop three alternate plans, based on the severity of the cuts. This was done without the knowledge of the general student affairs staff, to avoid unnecessary anxiety. Some of the departments (such as the child-care center, the residence halls, and the student union) are exempt from the cuts because as auxiliaries, they do not receive state funds. The department heads who are subject to the cuts have submitted their plans to the CSAO, according to guidelines set by her. These guidelines were to eliminate new purchases and travel and to cut student employees, part-time staff, and clerical personnel before full-time professional staff. Now, the student affairs manager has a discussion with the department heads, and after considerable debate, she decides that recreation and the health service will assume a larger share of the cut than will admissions and financial aid. This reflects the need of the college to attract students as well as the CSAO's plan to increase user fees for recreation and the health service. She is well aware of the inequity created between staff working in auxiliaries who are exempt from the cuts and those in other departments who are not. She has asked the directors of the auxiliary departments to make positions available to some of the staff who may have to be terminated by the state-funded areas. However, the CSAO also knows that this part of her plan may not be acceptable to the other vice presidents, since they may not have auxiliary operations in their divisions to protect their staff.

Once the student affairs leader has reached an agreement

with her directors about the way her division will handle the required deficit, she asks them to keep the plan confidential until she has met with the other vice presidents and the president. Since a decision at this meeting could reduce or increase the proposed cuts in student affairs, she does not want to inform staff about their status until she is certain about the final outcome. She is fortunate to work for a president who insists that the vice presidents work as a team, so that prearranged coalitions to protect certain budgets are not tolerated. Being confident of her plan for the student affairs division, she can present it to the management team knowing that it will be considered on its merits. She also realizes that any exaggerations of the negative consequences of cuts in her division will damage her credibility. She must show a willingness to share in the unpleasant task of accepting the cuts. Once the institutional decision is made, the CSAO should inform the directors, who in turn should meet with their staff to inform them. She should assure all staff that she is available to meet with them to hear their appeals. She knows that staff morale will be low for some time, and that she will need to do all she can to show appreciation for their efforts. She must also be prepared for negative reactions from students, and should meet with key student leaders to make sure they understand the plan and the rationale for it.

All budget deficits are difficult for institutions, but a severe mid-year cut is even more troublesome. Student affairs managers must rely on the trust they have built over time with staff, students, and administrative colleagues. They must understand the finances of their divisions very well, and they must make a realistic assessment of the consequences of cuts in each area. They should be honest and persuasive regarding their plans, and must show sensitivity to the needs of staff. Finally, they must be strong enough to withstand the inevitable criticism that accompanies such cutbacks and to encourage staff to continue their positive work with students.

Facing Resistance to Change. In this illustration, a newly appointed CSAO at a private college finds a reasonably satisfied staff who are comfortable doing things the same way they have done them for years. No new departments have been added, no grant proposals have been submitted, no assessment program exists, no external evaluations have been conducted, and (not surprisingly) few people on the campus look to the student affairs division for any innovative programs. Perhaps most disturbing to the new CSAO is the fact that the composition and interests of the student body have changed in the past ten years, but corresponding changes in student affairs programs, policies, and facilities have not occurred. The student affairs leader is new to the college and was hired by the president with the understanding that significant improvements needed to take place. The student affairs staff is not very enthusiastic about the new CSAO, since they had lobbied for the appointment of an internal candidate, a person who has been on the staff for almost twenty years. During the interview process, many of the student affairs staff boasted about the high quality of their programs, observations that the new CSAO noted were not shared by other administrators and faculty members. The student affairs leader views this situation as a tremendous challenge and is eager to initiate changes that can improve the college. How does he proceed?

Eagerness and impatience in managers, especially when coupled with staff resistance, can lead to authoritarianism. As Ehrle and Bennett (1988, p. 191) found in their study of academic managers, "Authoritarian postures can for a while masquerade as leadership, but in the long run, will be uncovered as lacking authenticity." This is the most important temptation this newly appointed CSAO must resist—to impose his will on the staff without their consent or participation. It simply will not work. Professionals do not respond well to orders from anyone. Unless the situation is so fraught with bitterness and strife that it is intolerable, it could also be a mistake for the new CSAO to terminate several key staff immediately and replace them with his own people. When this is done, it almost always results in worse problems than existed before. Trust is broken, anxieties are raised, and staff confidence is shattered. Moreover, the public scrutiny that accompanies such actions often obscures the intended results and focuses the college's attention primarily on the problems in the student affairs division.

The effective manager in this institution knows that patience and planning are required to make real changes. The process will be slower than the CSAO would like, but there is no other realistic choice. All the departments cannot change at once, and little will happen if the student affairs manager expects the entire division to improve overnight. The most effective approach, as Kouzes and Posner (1987) suggest, is to "plan small wins." By concentrating efforts on specific projects that are likely to achieve success, a series of minor advancements can be made that over a period of time will add up to very visible improvements. The admissions director may not have to be replaced nor the staff completely reorganized in order to improve performance. If special funds are provided for a new high school relations program, if a new staff member is hired to recruit honors students, or if a new computer link is established with the financial aid office, the staff will probably begin to sense some excitement and see that improvements can be made.

The CSAO must understand that real reform must occur from within departments, as a result of the creative efforts of the staff themselves, not as a function of external pressures. The student affairs leader should inspire staff to improve by "modeling the way" (Kouzes and Posner, 1987) in program development, policy formulation, and team building. Thus a very important task for student affairs managers is to present a vision to the staff of where they want to go, and to convince them they can get there. If this can be done in a manner that excites and challenges them, as opposed to insulting or threatening them, the CSAO will have accomplished a great deal in his effort to improve performance.

Instant greatness may be the dream of the newly appointed student affairs leader, but overcoming resistance to change and realizing actual improvements take time and careful planning. The peak of the mountain is reached not by a giant leap, but by a long series of carefully planned small steps.

The Effective Student Affairs Manager: Suggestions for Good Practice

CSAOs are responsible for people, programs, money, policy, and facilities. The ability to manage effectively is a major factor in their success. While they need to adjust their management practices to the distinct nature of their institutions, there are a number of characteristics of good management for CSAOs that apply to all. The following suggestions for good practice are presented.

Study the Environment. Student affairs leaders cannot be effective managers unless they know and understand their institutions and the many smaller communities of students and faculty they comprise. Detailed information about the student body, its quality, diversity, attitudes, and aspirations should be collected, studied, and shared on a regular basis. The CSAO should be an expert on the ecology of the campus, and needs to understand the subtleties of how groups of students and faculty interact and what their real experiences are. Comparative data about students from other, similar colleges and universities should be well known, and should be used as an aid in deciding priorities and policies. Effective programs and policies must recognize the specific needs of diverse groups.

Be Clear About Objectives. Cooperation and teamwork are essential to achieve success in student affairs, but CSAOs must know where they want to go and how to get there. In other words, to be effective managers, student affairs leaders must be clear about the direction they intend to take. This requires careful thought and planning, as well as extensive professional experience and knowledge. They should have a passionate commitment to the educational and social outcomes they desire for students, without imposing a rigid model on their staff or their institutions. Their enthusiasm for what student life can be should inspire others to become more productive professionals. As we saw earlier, aggressive leadership in charting a direction—as opposed to following a reactive, passive course—is good management in student affairs.

Enable Others to Be Successful. Kouzes and Posner (1987, p. 10) found that managers who were able to get extraordinary things done in their organizations were those who made it possible for others to do good work. This is especially true for

CSAOs, whose very business is people. Effective student affairs managers create opportunities for staff and others to grow and to learn. Enabling others to act is a critical component of their success as managers. They recognize that most improvements in educational programs for students result from "bottom-up" efforts of staff and not from "top-down" activities (Gilley, Fulmer, and Reithlingsbroefer, 1986, p. 86). Thus they derive their satisfaction as managers from the successes they see their staff, students, and institutions achieve, and talk very little about what they have done themselves. But student affairs leaders take the major responsibility for risks, while reassuring staff that their creative efforts are valued and appreciated.

Keep the Organization Flexible. CSAOs need to organize their programs and staff so that they can achieve their goals. However, they should never allow the organizational structure they create to become an end in itself. As Bolman and Deal (1984, p. 300) found in their extensive studies of managers, a fundamental requirement of effective leadership in complex organizations is flexibility. Needs change among students and new priorities are established by institutions. Many new functions have been added to the student affairs divisions of colleges and universities in recent years, ones not previously considered part of the traditional student affairs portfolio. The CSAO must be very sensitive to such changes, often anticipating them before others do and adjusting the policies, programs, and organizational structure of the division to meet the emerging needs. The inability or unwillingness of student affairs managers to adjust their organizations in this way can lead other divisions of the campus to assume responsibility for them.

Exercise Fiscal Integrity. As the primary administrator of a major component of the university, the CSAO is responsible for all financial matters in the student affairs division. This includes the acquisition, allocation, and accountability of all funds. Much of the success of the division depends on the ability of the CSAO to obtain the necessary financial resources. This requires good planning, persuasive skills, and the ability to describe program needs in understandable language. The effective student affairs manager must also develop systems for allocating the available resources in ways that ensure fairness and reward merit in programs and staff performance. The method of allocating resources should be clearly understood by staff, and should be reasonably consistent with practices used in other parts of the institution. Salaries of staff should reflect institutional priorities, marketplace standards, and internal equity.

The process of deciding annual budgets should represent an opportunity to involve staff in decision making and to review departmental objectives. The CSAO may have professional staff whose primary assignment is to monitor the day-by-day financial matters for the division. Such individuals are extremely important for successful management in student affairs, but the CSAO remains responsible for all fiscal affairs in the division. The president never expects anyone but the CSAO to answer questions about financial matters within the student affairs division. It takes expertise and time to stay up to date on the financial condition and performance of each of the departments within the division, but this responsibility the CSAO cannot ignore. Nothing can damage the effectiveness of the student affairs leader more than inept fiscal management. Independent audits of each of the departments should be conducted on a regular basis, and the student affairs leader should work closely with the chief business officer to ensure that the fiscal policies and procedures are in conformity with institutional standards. The success of programs in the division depends on the fiscal integrity and accountability of the student affairs leader.

Stay Close to the People. In their classic study of successful companies, Peters and Waterman (1982, p. 13) found that the most effective managers remained close to the customer. This is especially important for CSAOs, whose primary "customers," of course, are the students. Student affairs leaders cannot be good managers by isolating themselves from students, safely tucked away and protected in a remote office by several layers of bureacracy. Such isolation may seem comfortable, but it inevitably results in administrators who hear only what their staff tell them, and who become remote and irrelevant to students. "Walking around management" takes time and usually results in the CSAO's hearing and seeing some blunt and unsatisfying aspects of student life. However, to be a good manager, the student affairs leader must spend a lot of time in public, listening to and observing the realities of the campus and community. Such immersion in the daily (and nightly) life of the students is likely to build credibility and respect for the CSAO as a manager who cares. It can also make student affairs leaders more confident and persuasive as managers because they know on a firsthand basis what the needs of students are. Staying close to the people sets an example that other student affairs staff are likely to emulate, too. Of course, CSAOs must be sensitive that their active participation with students does not usurp the' important roles of their staff, who have the most frequent contact with students. The good manager visits with students in settings where the actions and accomplishments of the student affairs staff can be acknowledged.

Recognize and Reward Good Efforts. As the manager of a large organization, the student affairs leader recognizes that an important responsibility is to find ways to motivate staff and to make them as creative and productive as possible. This is done most effectively by establishing work environments that are characterized by openness, trust, and cooperation. Staff deserve to know what is expected of them and how they will be evaluated. Perhaps most important, they must be convinced that their efforts and accomplishments will be appreciated. The most effective way to motivate staff, encourage their creativity and productivity, and maintain their high morale is to recognize and reward their good efforts and accomplishments. This does not mean that money or promotions must always be used as rewards or incentives. In most cases, professional staff will respond very positively if they simply know, on a day-to-day basis, that their work is noticed and valued. Other, more substantive forms of recognition are important, too, and when individuals are thanked publicly for their work, it can reinforce the bonds of community and the goals and values of the entire student affairs division. Kouzes and Posner (1987) refer to the "celebration of accomplishments" as a very important management practice. Most of the rewards in student affairs are intrinsic and subjective; they usually involve the satisfaction of observing growth, insight, or intellectual excitement in students. The most sensitive CSAOs recognize the subtleties of staff-student relationships, and reward those whose efforts have made a difference. Recognition must be genuine, however, and must be directed at those who support the best values of the campus community. This compels the CSAO to be in close touch with the staff, what they do, and how they are actually perceived by students, faculty, and colleagues. Nothing can harm a recognition program more severely than rewarding persons who are not perceived by the campus community as deserving.

Conduct Regular Assessments. It is important to stay close to the students by directly observing their behavior and listening to their thoughts, but the most effective student affairs leaders know that systematic and independent assessments of student attitudes and values are also essential to good management. As close as CSAOs and their staff may feel they are to students, there are almost always useful insights that can only be gained by a regular assessment program. Credible studies of campus life can uncover needs that were previously unknown to the staff, and they can form the basis for new initiatives. Any of the excellent instruments available on the market can also be used to obtain essential feedback on the way various programs and policies are perceived. Moreover, such efforts can provide persuasive documentation for program proposals and resource requests. And assessment programs can create important links to academic departments and to the chief academic officer, paving the way for cooperative efforts with faculty to address the needs of students. The CSAO cannot substitute data for personal judgment in the management of the division; however, the absence of a systematic assessment program is evidence that the student affairs leader is probably relying too much on anecdotal hunches and traditions in making decisions.

Use a Team Approach. The skilled CSAO is able to bring people together with common interests and talents to work on projects of value to the institution. The most effective way to build excellent programs and win support for policies is by using a team approach. The key concept, as identified by Kouzes and Posner (1987) in their leadership studies, is collaboration. The student affairs leader must know the talents of the staff and should develop good relationships with faculty, students, and others so that the best people can be brought together in project teams. Most of these teams can be ad hoc in nature, since they are usually asked to address a specific issue, write a grant proposal, suggest ways to improve a service, or plan a conference. Teams can encourage staff, faculty, and students to think of the campus as a whole, blurring the departmental differences that often separate people. They can also produce very creative, high-quality results, if the CSAO is able to attract excellent people to them and give them challenging assignments. But simply establishing teams is not enough; good managers pay attention to how the members interact, where they are going, and what resources they need. They also stay out of their way and allow them to act when appropriate.

Use Technology to Improve Services. Few student affairs leaders are highly sophisticated in computer technology. However, they are responsible for departments such as registration, financial aid, and admissions that depend heavily on the electronic processing of data. They also know that their ability to communicate with their students is critically important, and that students are most comfortable with television as their means of obtaining information. Most institutions have experts who can be of assistance, but the CSAO should consult with other colleges and the many private firms that can also be of help. This is an ongoing process, since improvements in technology take place so fast that a system can be out of date in less than three years. Primary considerations for the student affairs managers, of course, are cost and dependability. Will the investment pay off in lower costs, better security, or improved service? If it is installed, will it function well and will the students accept it? The good manager investigates and tests such matters thoroughly by personally visiting sites where actual working systems can be examined and compares them with competitors. The CSAO should also cooperate with the chief academic and business officers in selecting technologies that are compatible with the overall campus plan.

Because of their primary orientation toward students, there may be a tendency on the part of some student affairs officers not to pay careful attention to this critical management function. But they are asking for trouble if they think they can simply delegate this matter to expert staff members. Entire campuses now communicate by electronic mail, students use computers every day in classrooms and laboratories and in their residences, and students expect to receive fast and efficient services from their institutions. They get understandably irritated if they have to wait in long lines for financial aid, if their grades are not mailed out on time, if the health service does not process their insurance forms quickly, or if it takes a week to obtain a new meal card. The student affairs manager must assume responsibility for improving such problems, and usually this involves the application of technology.

Establish Trust. Managers of organizations cannot be successful unless they have the trust of all those with whom they work. Trust for student affairs leaders does not come with the position; they must earn it through their actions. Being a great speaker, having a charismatic personality, or possessing great intellectual skills are enviable assets for CSAOs; however, these assets are not necessary in establishing trust, and are never substitutes for it. Trust is earned by showing genuine concern for others, demonstrating honesty in all matters, and working hard. Policy commitments must be consistently enforced, program evaluations must reflect previously agreed-on objectives, and professional confidences must be kept. Because student affairs is such a personal business, it is almost impossible for the CSAO to establish trust with students without getting to know large numbers of them on a first-name basis. If students trust the student affairs leader as a person, support for policies and programs will follow much more easily. But if they view CSAOs as remote, impersonal bureaucrats who have never bothered to visit their residence hall, attend their club initiation, or talk with them in the union commons, then they will be very skeptical about them.

Student affairs leaders should have strong commitments to ethical practices, and should make sure that all staff members are familiar with the standards adopted by the professional associations. However, they should also know that the best way to raise the level of awareness and commitment to such standards is by discussion, not fiat. Staff and students usually become more interested in ethical questions involving their work when presented with situational dilemmas to consider in workshops than they do by listening to a lecture about a code of standards. Such efforts can make the principles in the codes of professional ethics in student affairs become more than bland statements in impressive-looking brochures. They also reinforce feelings of trust and contribute to the education of students in important ways.

Learn to Take the Heat. The CSAO position is not for someone seeking a quiet, prdictable, noncontroversial life. Despite good planning, the use of teams, good management skills, and even a supportive president, there is frequent turmoil and considerable stress. Time demands are incessant, and with the kinds of social, political, racial, and educational issues facing the campus, the CSAO is often confronted with difficult and emotionally charged problems. Student affairs leaders may find themselves blamed for actions of students over which they have very little control; they may incur the wrath of students and others when unpopular decisions are made; and they may discover that the support they have is only as secure as the most recent decision they made. To be good managers, they must realize that they need to learn how to take considerable heat from others. Very few people enjoy being criticized, especially when it is viewed as unjustified and when it is public in nature. Unless the CSAO is a strong and emotionally healthy person, such criticism and the stress of the position can be debilitating. Moreover, the effectiveness of student affairs officers will become diminished if they show the effects of pressure, because those who work with them may lose confidence in their leadership ability. While CSAOs should strive not to personalize the criticism that accompanies their jobs, their own engagement with people and the issues is often so intense that this is not possible.

There is no simple way to deal with the pressure and stress of the position, since people handle these problems differently. The important message for good student affairs managers is to recognize the stress, understand it as a given in the position, and appreciate the joys of the job while learning to live with the heat.

Insist on Excellence. Programs, policies, staff, and facilities will be judged by the campus community on the basis of their quality. Everything that happens in the student affairs division is ultimately a reflection of the CSAO. Without attempting to control every decision made, the student affairs leader can set high standards for the division and insist that excellence be pursued in all activities. It is very difficult to recover from a sloppy orientation program, a bad audit of residence hall finances, a public report about unhealthy conditions in the child-care center, or bureaucratic inefficiency in delivering financial aid. Students, faculty, parents, and others react to what they see and experience, not to what is claimed to be true by the CSAO. It is impossible, of course, to avoid all such problems, but the best way to ensure high quality in student affairs is for the top manager to insist on excellence. Many young staff are so eager to serve the needs of students and impress their supervisors that they often initiate more programs than they can monitor effectively. The result is frequently embarrassing when quantity is substituted for quality. The best student affairs managers understand the fine line between encouraging the creative efforts of staff and controlling everything that is done themselves. They also know, however, that poor-quality efforts damage the entire division, and that it is far better to do three things very well than nine in a mediocre fashion. Nowhere is this commitment to excellence more important than in the hiring of professional staff. The division will be perceived in large part by what the campus community thinks about the staff. As managers, CSAOs must work very hard to attract and retain the very best staff they can for their institutions. Their own success depends on the quality of the staff they hire. Most colleges and universities have made strong commitments to excellence in their academic programs in recent years. It is the responsibility of the CSAO to be a strong advocate for the same level of excellence in all areas of student affairs.

Demonstrate Compassion. Effective management of student affairs requires many specific skills as well as hard work, organizational ability, and integrity. But good administration in student affairs is not a mechanical process, consisting simply of planning and implementing policies and programs. Very few young people progress toward their educational goals on straight and uninterrupted paths; there are financial, academic, personal, and other problems along the way, as well as self-doubt and discouragement, disappointment, and failure. The best CSAOs reflect real feelings in their actions and demonstrate concern and compassion for students. Student affairs leaders cannot allow their emotions to rule their actions, but if they do not have their hearts in their work, they are missing the essence of the educational mission. Students are extremely perceptive, and they will know if the student affairs leader really cares by watching and listening. Demonstrating compassion for students is essential for good management, but it also provides the greatest opportunities for personal satisfaction for the CSAO.

A very important task for the student affairs manager is to try to persuade the entire campus community to reflect this genuine sense of caring. If he or she is successful, the students will benefit greatly and the institution may reflect a level of humaneness that enriches the academic life for everyone. Most experienced and successful CSAOs remain in their positions because of the rewards that come from personal interaction with students. This same compassion toward the student affairs staff is essential if they are to develop respect for the CSAO and continue to grow professionally.

Management of student affairs in higher education is a complex and often unpredictable task that requires thoughtful planning and sensitivity to others. It can be quite messy at times because of the highly volatile nature of student problems and campus issues. It is very demanding in terms of time and stress, but it can also provide great satisfaction when progress is made in student growth and development. CSAOs typically confront many management problems. Their ability to address these problems effectively is critical to their success as managers. The best are not those who experience the fewest problems; they are the ones who find realistic ways to deal with them successfully.

The next chapter addresses the second major role of the CSAO, that of mediator of disputes, conflicts, and disagreements.

6

The Mediator

Student affairs leaders are engaged in competition for resources, personnel, and facilities, yet they spend a considerable part of their time attempting to foster cooperation. They are faced with contradictory expectations from various groups, who often demand action to meet their service needs or political agendas. They may be expected by their staff to be forceful leaders, by the students to be sensitive peacemakers, and by the faculty to be passive support people. Their role is one of the most exciting in higher education; it focuses on the aspirations, interests, and achievements of students and thus inevitably confronts their frustrations, prejudices, and failures as well. CSAOs occupy the public stage, where the real-world concerns of students as people are acted out on a daily (and nightly!) basis. The job is messy, loud, joyful, agonizing, and important. The CSAO is expected by the president to give direction to and make sense out of the elusive and perplexing phenomenon called "student life."

Student affairs leaders must be effective managers of the various departments and programs under their jurisdiction, including the extensive financial responsibilities of the position. However, their ability to handle controversy, resolve conflicts, and foster cooperation among competing interests is equally important to their success. The CSAO is expected to be a problem solver, and with students being the focus of attention, this means dealing directly with their disputes, grievances, and frustrations. The most effective student affairs leaders are skilled mediators on their campuses and in their communities, and they use this skill to resolve disputes, to encourage cooperation, and to help others learn. The role of the CSAO as mediator is the subject of this chapter.

The Mediation Process

Mediation usually refers to formal, third-party intervention in disputes between opposing groups within organizations. It has become a very attractive alternative to more formal arbitration approaches and legal proceedings, because it frequently is less expensive, more informal, and less adversarial. It also presents opportunities for participant involvement and education, and can lead to long-term improvements in the resolution of differences. A great deal of attention has been given to mediation in the professional management literature in recent years, reflecting the emergence of innovative approaches and the increased sophistication of practitioners. Formal mediation processes have useful applications for student affairs administrators, but it is the informal applications of mediation principles that are most helpful. Student affairs leaders generally act as mediators in a variety of informal ways.

Because the issues CSAOs face are often volatile, it is important that they take skillful and sensitive approaches. Himes (1980, p. 229) has noted that "coercive or violent tactics often create emotional scars, a sense of anguish, and intense hostilities that linger long after the conflict episode has terminated." Such consequences can be very destructive to the social and educational climate of the campus, so that the CSAO must avoid the use of clumsy tactics, which by themselves may cause an already difficult situation to deteriorate. This requires a sensitivity to people and their needs, and a determination to find ways in which groups can share the power. CSAOs act as mediators who "interact in the conflict process itself; they do not remain in the wings" (Gerstein and Reagan, 1986, p. 57). Folberg and Taylor (1984, p. 335) argue that "mediation is premised on the desirability of making decisions by consent, not on the imposition of authority. . . . It can facilitate a norm that promotes cooperation and self-determination rather than coercion." Student affairs leaders will encounter great difficulty and resistance if they rely on what they may think is the bureaucratic authority of their positions to make decisions. As Kouzes and Posner (1987, p. 27) assert, "Leadership is in the eye of the follower. . . . Over time, those who would be followers will determine whether that person should be, and will be, recognized as a leader." It is possible to force others to do things, but effective leaders understand that they must find ways to encourage others to want to do things if they are to be successful.

CSAOs not only have a responsibility to solve problems and resolve conflicts, they also have an obligation to educate their students through the decision-making process. In spite of unpleasant incidents or bitter arguments, they must retain their basic trust in others and a faith that students are capable of resolving their differences. They must work hard to avoid what Yates (1985, p. 135) calls the development of an "enemy psychology," viewing certain students or groups as malevolent forces that are consciously seeking to undermine others' interests. This siege mentality can isolate the CSAO as a distant, authoritarian bureaucrat, making genuine attempts at mediation impossible. Being part of the campus conflict process, student affairs leaders can be viewed as "shock absorbers" (Gilmore, 1988, p. 10), mediating between groups and often serving as buffers for the various pressures that are exerted. They do not always have to protect the president from the sometimes nasty demands of student groups, but they can interpret messages and can open lines of communication that may appear to be closed.

Student affairs administrators often see students and others when they are under stress, when they are angry, or when they feel threatened. As a result, they must be keen observers of others' behavior and patient listeners as well. As Folberg and Taylor (1984, p. 194) propose, they should strive to "use mediation as a format for the ventilation of negative feelings, allowing decisions to emerge based on fairness, rather than only on the letter of the law." They are also faced with the reality that when groups are vying with one another, a "win-lose mentality" (Blake and Mouton, 1984, p. 9) may come to replace necessary cooperation and problem solving. Each group may have a vested interest in its own success, even if one group's gain is at the expense of the other. Moreover, if they expect further conflict, neither group can visualize alternatives to continued antagonism and hostility.

Student affairs administrators often are caught between the need to control a conflict situation and their desire to address the underlying tension that created the conflict in the first place. They are confident they can mediate the conflict and get the participants on both sides to deal constructively with the root causes of the problems, but time does not permit this luxury. They recognize that superficial control-oriented decisions do not resolve differences and often lead to increased tension because of the way in which they were handled. As Gray (1989, p. 276) suggests, "Institutional commitments are needed to construct forums whereby groups and individuals can participate together in making cooperative decisions." Thus, the CSAO should work to gain the understanding of the president, the vice presidents, and other key staff that certain conflicts will take time to resolve and are not effectively handled by authoritarian approaches. There are limits, of course, and taking too much time may subject the student affairs leader to harsh criticism for being indecisive. This is a dilemma all experienced student affairs administrators are familiar with, and they must become good judges of what the tolerable level of expectations is on each issue faced.

CSAOs do not succeed as mediators of conflicts and disputes simply by calling angry groups together and encouraging them to talk. They do not need to follow all the elaborate procedures used by professional mediators in typical labor-management disputes, but they should have a plan and a strategy based on successful approaches described in the mediation literature. For example, the seven-step process outlined by Folberg and Taylor (1984, p. 32) includes specific tasks for which each group must assume responsibility, as well as very helpful suggestions for writing, clarifying, and reviewing the negotiated decision. Fisher and Ury (1983) present a strategy for negotiation based on studies at the Harvard Mediation Project. It is designed to help mediators "get to yes" with conflicting groups, without litigation or coercion. In the six-stage "Interface Conflict Resolving model" used by Blake and Mouton (1984, p. 18), step 1 of the process requires each group to work separately to create an optimal model specific to its problems and needs. These writers suggest that the key parts of their approach are that "(1) active participation is essential to support any changes, (2) those who have the problem can themselves learn to diagnose the causes underlying it, and (3) reliance should be placed on insights, understanding, and agreement by the members themselves as the basis for problem solving rather than on coercion, compromise, or capitulation" (Blake and Mouton, 1984, p. 77). Student affairs leaders should also know that there is considerable evidence (for example, Ury, Brett, and Goldberg, 1988, p. xiii) that an effectively applied mediation program can improve the overall climate of organization and resolve disputes in ways that promote understanding. Moreover, as Yates (1985, pp. 130–131) argues in his political analysis of organizations, "The purpose of mediation is to bring the normal function of bureaucratic politics out into the open and thereby avoid backstairs intrigue, end runs, covert alliances, and other manoeuvres well known to shrewd bureaucratic politicians." Student affairs leaders can seriously damage the trust they are so dependent on if they use a clandestine, politically oriented way of making decisions and settling disputes.

CSAOs should also be aware of the considerable educational potential the mediation process can have for students who participate as well as for those who are simply campus observers. The process used in settling disputes may be just as important as the eventual decision. Student affairs administrators often transmit stronger messages to students by the way they approach problems than they do by the actual policy outcomes. If they can help students learn effective ways of dealing with differences and resolving their problems in a humane manner, they will have contributed in very important ways to their education. As Folberg and Taylor (1984, p. ix) note, it is possible to train people to foster the constructive rather than the destructive potential in conflicts. In short, student affairs leaders must always remember their educational role, even in the heat and pressure of having to settle conflicts.

Issues in Mediation

Student affairs leaders must be sensitive readers of the campus and its many smaller communities. They should be ahead of others in understanding and anticipating the concerns of diverse groups. They should also become sophisticated about the special ways that the various smaller communities on their campuses have of dealing with their concerns. The most successful CSAOs know that certain approaches to resolving problems will not work with some groups, because of tradition, culture, or other factors. Becoming effective mediators requires careful consideration of several issues by CSAOs.

Conflicting Expectations. Although this is surprising, it is not unusual for CSAOs to have serious misunderstandings about what is expected of them. This is especially true of new administrators who have not had extensive experience in student affairs. An advertised job description may only have emphasized line responsibility for several departments as well as the need for programs and services in support of the academic mission. During the interview process, no one, including the president, may have said anything about campus conflicts and disputes. The candidate might have been hired on the basis of demonstrating an impressive knowledge of higher education, of student development theory, and of program strategy. However, just after he or she takes the job, there could be several volatile student-related disputes on the campus, and the CSAO might be completely unprepared to deal with them. Worse, the student affairs leader might not understand that the campus community (especially the president) expected him or her to solve them. When the inevitable criticism arises in such situations, it is not surprising for the CSAO to feel resentment: "No one told me I was expected to do these things. I'm not a boxing referee or a district judge . . . I'm an educator!" In the rough-and-tumble world of student affairs, such administrators do not last very long. This

underscores the fact that well in advance of the initial appointment date, the president and the CSAO must have a good understanding about what is expected of the student affairs leader.

Avoidance and Denial. Experienced CSAOs will immediately
recognize the problem of avoidance and denial in dealing with
campus disputes. It is what Daniels and Spiker (1987, p. 175)
refer to as "smoothing": the process of avoidance or suppres-
sion, where administrators and others pretend that the sources
of conflict are not present in the hope that the conflict will dissi-
pate on its own. One of the responsibilities of student affairs
leaders in their role as mediators is to have the courage to bring
problems out into the open and to confront them honestly. They
may receive lots of advice from colleagues to leave certain problems alone, because there are fears about what the consequences
might be if they are dealt with. Moreover, if the student affairs
leaders are the ones who initiate public discussions of sensitive
and controversial issues, and the subsequent outcomes prove
embarrassing for the institution, they are very likely to incur
the wrath of colleagues who warned them to leave the problem
alone. More than one CSAO has lost a job because of such actions, especially when they have been expected to settle the
conflict and were not able to. All of these difficult circumstances
tempt student affairs leaders to avoid conflicts and to deny that
they are serious problems. But such behavior almost always
backfires, since problems that are ignored often fester and eventually have to be faced because they get so bad that they virtually burst on the scene. Then CSAOs are in serious trouble,
because the problem is more difficult to deal with, and they may
find themselves being blamed by the president and others for
not anticipating the major consequences earlier. A failure to
recognize campus stress among students, an unwillingness to
deal openly with student health issues, or a denial that serious
racial conflicts exist among various student groups are examples of problems, that, if denied, can often lead to very serious
and negative repercussions. Of course, when they confront those
issues, CSAOs must have the courage and the mediation skills
to deal with them effectively.

CSAOs are often asked by presidents and others about potential problems and conflicts, and they should resist the temptation to tell them only what is pleasant and positive. Some insecure student affairs administrators may think that it is their responsibility to assure their presidents that everything is fine; they may fear that admitting the presence of conflicts on the campus is evidence that they are not doing their jobs well. In fact, though, they should be tuned in to the real world of the students and to share what they see and know. They are expected to create a climate where conflicts can be addressed openly, and of course they are also expected to see to it that these conflicts are resolved.

Fence-Sitting. Another important issue for CSAOs to consider in their role as mediators is "fence-sitting" — finding themselves in the middle of the problem. As Gerstein and Reagan (1986, p. 67) assert, "When mediators are in the middle between two parties in conflict, a pretense of neutrality or altruism is seldom believed for long, and may perpetuate a continued state of distrust." This is often a dilemma for student affairs leaders: Do they expose their own views and argue for a solution that may be right but that one of the groups will not appreciate? Are student affairs administrators real people with ideas and beliefs, or are they simply impersonal bureaucrats who apply various mediation techniques to campus problems? Will they be perceived as unconcerned and uncommitted if they always remain "on the fence"? Can they stand up to the often bitter criticism they will receive from outraged groups who find their neutrality unacceptable?

Few campus issues are so well defined that all of the morality falls with only one group; usually there are good arguments and legitimate grievances on both sides, and so it is not easy or advisable for CSAOs to assert their own point of view. Presidents and other administrators may grow impatient with CSAOs if they see "fence-sitting" as not resolving the issue quickly enough or in the direction they want it to take.

The following example may illustrate the fence-sitting dilemma for the student affairs leader. When plans are made for

the yearly campuswide convocation, the Hispanic Student Association is invited, along with several other student groups, to be
represented in the official platform ceremonies and to present
a report on its activities to the university community. This is
matter involving considerable prestige, but two different Hispanic student groups approach the CSAO, each insisting that
only their organization actually represents the 2,500 Hispanic
students at the institution. The two factions have serious differences about their views of politics, history, and culture, and there
is open hostility between them. The campus newspaper makes
this dispute public, and now there is widespread awareness of
the conflict with the convocation program, which is only three
weeks away. The CSAO knows that she must resolve the problem and has strong feelings of her own that one of the groups
is more deserving of recognition than the other. Does she "sit
on the fence" between the two, not exposing her feelings, simply trying to get them to decide? Or if she asserts her own beliefs, what are the consequences for the group that loses and
feels it was coerced? Can she live with these and other negative
consequences? Will she be given time to solve the problem in
a civil manner, or will she be perceived as a weak administrator if she does not solve it? The CSAO will benefit in situations
like this by connecting with staff and faculty who are familiar
with the issue. She should also be prepared to offer alternative
solutions to the two student groups that enable both of them
to retain their dignity.

There is no prescription for effective mediation practices
in every campus situation. CSAOs must try to understand when
it is advantageous to "sit on the fence" and when it is necessary
to get off it. They must also think carefully about the likely consequences of both options.

Stirring Things Up. Student affairs administrators have a very
important educational role, and most of them are convinced that
students learn more about themselves, about others, and about
leadership when campus life is full of debate, discussion, and
the lively exchange of ideas. CSAOs should not be timid about
encouraging students to engage in programs and projects that

may lead to conflict with others. If the campus is not characterized by much debate about important social and political issues,
the student affairs leader may deliberately attempt to stir things
up. By inviting groups to share their views about their experiences, by raising questions about policies, by arranging conferences on various issues, or by inviting challenging speakers,
CSAOs can raise the level and the intensity of campus debate
and discussion. Of course, after stirring things up, CSAOs may
have to spend many long hours mediating the very conflicts they
encouraged in the first place!

If CSAOs are comfortable about their role on the campus,
and confident in their ability to mediate problems, their efforts
to create a little turmoil will pay educational dividends. Some
student affairs leaders may prefer to stay in the background,
out of the limelight, and out of the editorial column of the student newspaper, thinking that their job is to keep the campus
as quiet as possible. But this approach clashes with their professional obligations for students' education. Students are not served
well by protecting them from ideas, criticism, and intellectual
scrutiny. The best student affairs administrators are well known
and visible on their campuses, known for their strong commitments and principles and their willingness to challenge students'
assumptions and beliefs. They are not passive, neutral, non-
participants whose views are a mystery to students. CSAOs need
to decide if they are confident enough in their mediation skills
and comfortable enough with their presidents and administrative colleagues to stir things up in this way. The conflict and
criticism they will inevitably have to face must be weighed
against the benefits of creating some intellectual turmoil.

When to Intervene. When conflicts occur between student groups,
or when a student organization confronts the chairperson of an
academic department on a policy issue, the natural tendency
on the part of the CSAO may be to rush over and settle the
matter as quickly as possible. This may be especially true of
inexperienced student affairs leaders, who are anxious to demonstrate their effectiveness as problem solvers and are determined
not to be accused of being unresponsive. Some insecure CSAOs

may also be seeking a visible "victory" to win the confidence or approval of their presidents, and thus may try to get the personal credit for solving the dispute. But it is often a mistake to intervene directly when a conflict first becomes known. Experienced CSAOs are interested in settling the dispute in a humane and fair manner, but they are also mindful that the campus is watching and that the way it is handled can have important consequences for the climate of the institution. They are keenly aware, too, that they are not serving the educational needs of students well by making them depend on someone else to solve their problems and grievances. If the student affairs leader moves in quickly, takes over the situation, and settles it, students on one side of the issue may for a time think he is a hero, but such actions contribute little to their learning, and do not create positive conditions for future conflict resolution.

Knowing when to intervene in a dispute requires sensitivity to students and a sound familiarity with the issues involved. Effective "mediation" by a student affairs leader in some cases may simply mean allowing the disagreeing groups to continue their debate until they resolve it themselves. It may also mean having informal discussions with individuals involved in the matter, helping them to clarify their thinking and consider their options. Intervention does not have to mean formal mediation at the table with the elected leaders of opposing groups. If the CSAO is convinced that a situation is so volatile or dangerous that the groups cannot be allowed to meet by themselves, then personal intervention is obviously needed. However, most campus disputes are more subtle than that, and need careful scrutiny before intervention is made.

Even the most active student affairs administrators cannot know the detailed agendas and priorities of all student groups, and thus must frequently rely on faculty, staff, and community members for advice on how to proceed. To seek advice from others is not a sign of weakness, as some inexperienced CSAOs may think, but a necessary and important step in the process of understanding campus conflicts.

Who Should Be Involved? In their zeal to prove their effectiveness, some CSAOs may try to resolve conflicts on their own.

But few problems are so simple that they can be settled by one person, and few student affairs leaders are so skilled that they can solve problems by themselves. Many campus conflicts linger because the student affairs leader has not found or used the most effective people to help solve them. In some cases, the most obvious person, at least in terms of their job title, may not be the best one to invite into discussions about the dispute, because the timing may not be right or the person may not be trusted by others. Knowing who to involve requires sensitivity to the problems and a knowledge of the participants and their needs. CSAOs must accept the fact that they cannot resolve all campus conflicts, especially those in areas where they do not have decision-making authority (such as with respect to grades assigned by faculty). However, they do have a responsibility to work toward methods of resolving differences on the campus that are open and humane.

An approach to mediating disputes that can be quite successful is for the CSAO to train small groups of faculty, staff, and students to serve as "conflict resolution teams." These teams can become very effective in addressing special problems on the campus, and if they gain acceptance, they can serve as models for settling disputes. Few teams can be equally good at all problems, and so it is likely that each will develop its own special expertise. Their focus may be on health, political, religious, or ethnic conflicts. CSAOs can greatly extend their commitments to the mediation process as the model for resolving campus conflicts by the use of such teams. These teams require a good deal of attention and need considerable training, but have excellent potential for improving the ways problems are resolved. Moreover, they offer very constructive ways to involve others in important tasks.

Some problems and conflicts may become sufficiently difficult that consideration should be given to inviting professional mediators to the campus to help resolve them. Business and industry have followed such practices for many years, and colleges and universities could certainly benefit from doing the same. Such organizations as the National Institute for Dispute Resolution and the Society of Professionals in Dispute Resolution (Folberg and Taylor, 1984, pp. 357–358) offer services that

can be very useful. "Celebrity mediation" may also be an op
tion, inviting to the campus a well-known public figure who by
reason of charisma or reputation may help settle a very difficult
situation. The University of Michigan used this approach successfully in 1989 when it invited the Reverend Jesse Jackson
to help in the mediation process on grievances between African-
American students and the university administration. Other
CSAOs may want to involve university attorneys in their efforts
to settle problems. Many of these professionals have specific
training and skills that can make their participation helpful.
While inviting persons from outside the campus to help mediate problems is very infrequently done, it can assure participants the institution is serious about the matter and that the
mediator is not predisposed to favor either side.

Ethical Dilemmas. Student affairs leaders often find themselves
in the middle on campus issues — between the president and the
student government, between a student and a faculty member,
or between two student groups. As discussed earlier, "fence-
sitting" can have its advantages, since it may enable CSAOs
to communicate openly with both sides, while not aligning themselves with either on the issue itself. However, being in the middle also presents some potential conflicts for student affairs administrators. For example, the president of a college may insist
on refusing to recognize the Gay Student Alliance as a student
organization, despite the outraged protests of the student group
and even the arguments of the legal staff. The CSAO believes
the college should recognize the group and supports its right
to organize; however, the president is convinced that to do so
will damage the college's fund-raising potential and its support
in the legislature. The CSAO is caught in the middle, with an
ethical dilemma — should her commitment be to the institution
and its needs, or to her belief that the student group has a right
to be recognized? In another example, the student affairs leader
may be in the middle between two student political groups who
are in a bitter dispute about how student fees should be allocated by student government. The dispute has extended over
a period of several weeks, which has delayed the allocations,

including the annual funds granted to the athletic association. The CSAO is working to mediate the dispute between the two student groups, is convinced that it will be resolved in another three weeks, and most important, feels that the participating students are learning a great deal from the process and will eventually settle the matter themselves. However, the student affairs leader is informed by the athletic director that the allocations must be made in one week, or booster support for the new stadium may be lost. Thus, the CSAO is caught in the middle again with an ethical dilemma—how does he weigh his commitment to the students and their learning against the need of the athletic department to get its money?

Very few conflicts on the campus will be entirely free of ethical considerations for student affairs leaders. Some, such as the two examples just cited, present very perplexing dilemmas that are not easy to resolve. Moreover, there is no simple prescription to follow that will reveal the "correct" response in all situations. As mediators of campus conflicts with students, CSAOs can only be successful if they have the trust of everyone involved. This requires that they be absolutely honest in all of their contacts with students. It is better to share the dilemmas described earlier in an open and forthright manner than it is to conceal information from students or to try to hoodwink them. If students and others discover that the process was not completely honest, then the effectiveness of the CSAO as a mediator is gone.

In the actual process of mediating differences between groups, it is not unusual for tempers to flare and for individuals to say some very inflammatory things about others. Because some issues are so explosive, many people who are not involved in the face-to-face efforts to settle the dispute are very interested in what is being said. This is often true of the media and of institutional and community officers who feel they have a stake in the outcome. The CSAO has an important obligation to protect the confidentiality of the discussions. Knowing that open expression of feelings is necessary to resolve most issues, CSAOs also understand that revealing the details of such delicate conversations to outsiders may destroy any attempt to settle the conflict. The CSAO must maintain the trust of the participants in the process by upholding the confidential nature of the discussions, despite the considerable pressure from non-participants.

Student affairs leaders need to be effective mediators if they are to succeed in their positions. They also need to think carefully about the various issues raised by their involvement in mediating conflicts, some of which may be particular to their institution. They must be comfortable with their role in relation to the president and the other administrative officers of the institution, knowing that their support and understanding of the process is present. They must also give thoughtful consideration to any ethical dilemmas they encounter in their role as conflict resolvers, and be open about these matters with others.

Case Studies of Problems Needing Mediation

To illustrate how CSAOs may actually work to settle disputes, some brief case studies follow.

A Fraternity Racial Conflict. At this private college, the fraternities have been the major locus of weekend social activity for decades, and are almost exclusively white. African-American students do not attend these fraternity-based social activities, preferring to gather in off-campus facilities. One of the fraternities conducted a party with a very derogatory racial theme, with most of the students in attendance dressed in ways depicting negative stereotypes of African Americans. A newspaper reporter was present, took some pictures at the party, and published a story of the event in the city paper. It was quickly picked up by the wire services, and a great deal of damaging publicity was given to the college throughout the state. The Black Student Alliance was outraged, and threats of violent retaliation against the fraternity were rumored on the campus. The CSAO was presented with angry petitions from faculty, students, and community groups demanding that the fraternity be immediately expelled from the campus. At the same time, the fraternity apologized for any problems it may have caused and claimed it had no intention of insulting anyone. Its leaders also informed the student affairs office that the fraternity had retained an attorney to support its assertion that the college has no right to regulate what it considers free speech on its own property. The college had made a major commitment five years ago to increase its minority enrollment and to improve the racial climate on the campus. The number of African-American students at the college had more than doubled during this period, and the president is determined that this incident be resolved so that this progress will not be deterred. What does the CSAO do?

The student affairs leader has done her homework. She has good relations with the fraternity and with the Black Student Alliance. She knows the officers personally, has attended some of their functions, and is trusted by both groups. She also has the support of the president, who has seen her demonstrate her effectiveness in settling other campus problems, and so she does not have to face authoritarian, coercive orders from her boss to settle the matter immediately. Moreover, his confidence in her provides a very necesary buffer from the demands being made by others. She also knows the faculty advisers to these student organizations, and as part of her efforts to improve the racial climate at the college, had established a faculty advisory council to address campus problems. Both of these faculty advisers were active participants on the council. Perhaps most important, she had developed four "campus mediation teams" in the past three years, each composed of two students and two faculty members. They had received extensive training in helping to resolve disputes, and were well accepted on the campus. Within twenty-four hours of the incident, she had visited personally with the leaders of the Black Student Alliance, the fraternity, the faculty advisory council, the president, the student affairs staff, the campus police, and one of the campus mediation teams. She knew it was important to resolve the problems to avoid any violence, but she also knew that the way the conflict was approached would have important implications for the college's efforts to attract African-American students and improve the racial climate.

Because the students knew her and trusted her, they

agreed to her proposal to have the campus mediation team, along with two trusted student affairs staff members, meet with each group separately to assess their feelings and expectations. Then, each group designated four representatives to participate with members of the mediation team in face-to-face discussions at an off-campus location. The CSAO did not attend but saw to it that meals and other needs were provided for. She decided she should not be a direct participant herself because she knew she might have to intervene if the process she set up did not work. She also wanted to reinforce the role of the campus mediation team as a workable model in resolving such disputes. She gave no specific deadline to the groups, but did tell them they should expect the process to take some time.

The team and the student organization representatives met seven times over the next two weeks. They were under great pressure from people who demanded action, but they were assured by the CSAO that they had her support. She in turn assured the president that the process was necessary and that it was proceeding smoothly. The campus mediation team developed a written agreement with recommended sanctions and public statements from each group, and suggested an elaborate education-awareness plan for the fraternity system. The CSAO met with the team, clarified and confirmed their plan, and indicated her support for it. She immediately shared it with the president and informed hm that she was ready to accept it. Along with the campus mediation team, the faculty advisers, and two student affairs staff members, she then called meetings with the entire membership of each organization, allowing the officers to explain the agreement, the process used to achieve it, and the plan for further education. After this was done, the presidents of the two organizations held a joint campus press conference to announce the results of the effort. Of course, not everyone was entirely satisfied with the outcome, but most were; violence was averted, and the process used encouraged the open exchange of ideas and invited positive follow-up activities.

The CSAO knows that to be successful, this agreement is only one stage in a mediation-education process that has to continue for some time. She, the campus mediation team, the faculty advisory council, and the student organization officers must continue their conversations for several weeks. She has taken a good deal of criticism regarding this controversy, including an accusation that if she had developed a good education-awareness program years ago, the incident would have never taken place. However, she was able to set in motion a process for resolving this conflict between the two student groups while maintaining the integrity of the college, the support of the president, and the trust of the students. She was a very successful mediator in this situation.

Police Department Insensitivity. In this example, the student government association presents the CSAO with a lengthy list of grievances concerning the campus police department. It is alleged that the police enforce the laws inconsistently, are insensitive to the special needs of foreign students, women, and minorities, overcharge student groups for security at special events, and are unprofessional and authoritarian. The police chief, who reports to the vice president for administration, has responded to the complaints with anger, being quoted in the campus newspaper as saying that the students are wealthy, selfish, and disrespectful of authority. He strongly resents the public criticism of his officers, claiming that the students do not understand the kinds of pressures they face every day. In particular, he refuses to speak with the student body president, who has made several negative statements about the police.

Security on the campus and in the community is a very serious issue, and students and parents have expressed their concerns about it to the college administration. There have been several assaults on campus during the year, and thefts and burglary have increased significantly. The president is very concerned about safety for students and employees, and does not want an image of an unsafe campus to discourage prospective applicants. The grievances presented by the student government association have received considerable publicity, and the president informs the CSAO and the vice president for administration that this problem must be solved as quickly as possible.

To complicate matters further, the student government

association purposely presented its grievances to the CSAO, even though it was aware the police department reports to the vice president for administration. The student leaders view the administrative vice president as distant and unresponsive and have said she is part of the problem. This has caused this officer to express anger at the CSAO, who she suspects may have contributed to the grievances being presented. These two administrators have been able to work together reasonably well for the past five years, but this incident has clearly strained their relations. The CSAO is thus faced with the list of student grievances, the concerns about campus safety, a resentful police chief, a defensive vice presidential colleague, and the president's expectation that the problem will be solved quickly, without damage to the institution's image. What should the student affairs leader do?

Despite some previous friction, the CSAO and the vice president for administration must work together to solve this problem. If they are fighting each other, the problem will get worse, will end up in the president's office, and both of them will be held accountable and may lose their jobs. Thus, the first step for the student affairs leader is to have a frank conversation with the administrative vice president to arrive at a strategy to address this conflict. This will require that the chief administrative officer acknowledge that the grievances presented by the students represent real concerns, which may entail some prodding by the CSAO. In previous months, the student affairs leader had talked with the administrative officer about the students' complaints and had made a number of suggestions to improve the situation. However, these suggestions were ignored, and student requests to meet with the police were rejected. Now, the administrative vice president is looking to the student affairs officer for help. She says, "I don't like to get involved in these student problems." However, both administrators must assume responsibility for them, and if it takes a visit with the president, this must be accomplished before any other actions are initiated.

The two vice presidents held separate meetings with the student leaders and the chief of police to assess the situation more carefully. After doing this, they agreed that the grievances were serious, and that the level of trust was so low that any direct contact between the police and the student government association would be unproductive at this time. They were careful not to blame either side, and emphasized their desire to resolve the problems without identifying any losers or winners. Neither side was ready to meet with the other, and the police chief was not comfortable in sharing his real concerns with the two vice presidents, one of whom was his boss. Thus, the student affairs leaders suggested that four faculty members be invited to serve as a neutral, preliminary intervention team with both sides. The students and the police were each able to select faculty members from a pool of informal mediators the CSAO had organized a year ago. As a result, each side felt it was granted some role in the process, even in its initial stages. The faculty team met with each side in the dispute three times over a period of a week and listened to its concerns. The faculty team then asked each side to write a detailed description of what it considered to be an effective police-student relationship. When this task was completed, the papers were shared with the opposing groups, and considerable similarities were found. Both sides had made constructive suggestions for increased involvement, student feedback, officer and student awareness programs, and an advisory committee. The faculty team discussed the contents of both papers with each group, and assured each that it sensed a willingness on the other side to meet and begin direct efforts to resolve their differences.

The faculty team met with three representatives from each side, and found that the time spent with the groups in the past two weeks preparing them for a joint meeting had paid dividends. Using the papers they had written as a relatively safe way to begin their discussions, the faculty team encouraged the two groups to explore options and to avoid making accusations. The groups were assured that they were under no pressure to reach an agreement right away, and were informed that a series of meetings might be necessary before a solution could be found. The faculty team was delighted to find that the groups themselves had taken over most of the discussions and were assuming the responsibility for resolving the problems. In four rather lengthy meetings in an off-campus location, the two groups negotiated an agreement, and with the help of the faculty team, clarified it in a written plan that was submitted to the two vice presidents. The plan was accepted and the specific suggestions were implemented. It was recognized that the agreement would only be effective if there was extensive follow-up in the next several months. The groups involved in the mediation process agreed to continue biweekly meetings for the remainder of the year to monitor the progress of the plan.

The process set up by the CSAO to resolve this very difficult conflict took over three weeks of intensive work and involved the efforts of many people. However, it resulted in an agreement that has an excellent chance of improving police-student relations, it avoided ugly confrontations, and it did not label anyone as winners or losers. The mediation process also was instructive for the participants, since it showed them constructive ways of approaching future problems. And although not directly responsible for the police department, the CSAO was able to involve a reluctant vice presidential colleague in a process she was not used to, keep the problem out of the president's office, and retain the confidence of the students and the police. The student affairs leader did not serve directly as the principal mediator, but was the key person who made the process work for the benefit of the institution.

Student Harassment Charge. In this example, a female student filed a charge of sexual harassment against her male physics professor. In her written complaint to the CSAO, she alleged that the professor failed her in the course after she refused to have sexual relations with him. She felt so intimidated by the situation that she did not confront him, the department chair, or the college dean about the incident. It was only after considerable urging from her roommate that she reported the matter to the student affairs office. The CSAO listened to the student recount her experiences with the professor, arranged an appointment for her with a colleague in the counseling center, and confirmed with the student that she wanted to pursue the complaint.

The CSAO is the only female vice president, and her attempts to establish formal procedures for adjudicating sexual harassment charges on the campus have been unsuccessful. She has a good relationship with the chief academic officer, but he has been unwilling to push the seven college deans or the faculty into adopting a policy, since he correctly senses their resistance to it and is wary of losing their support. Moreover, there is a belief among the predominantly male faculty that such a policy would encourage female students to manipulate instructors to obtain higher grades. The CSAO has talked with the president about the need for a sexual harassment policy, but he has not wanted to "stir that kettle of worms."

The student affairs leader decided to discuss the student charges with the chief academic officer at once. She was able to get him to agree to conduct a quiet investigation of the matter, and he called the arts and sciences dean and asked him to talk with the chair of the physics department and the accused professor. Two days later, the chief academic officer informed the CSAO that he had inquired into the matter and the professor assured the dean that there was no basis for the charge and that the student had simply performed poorly in the class. The chief academic officer then said he knew the professor, took him and his academic colleagues at their word, and as far as he was concerned, the matter was closed.

The CSAO strongly objected, arguing that the student had not even been afforded a hearing, and if nothing else, the institution ought to be aware that the student could file a lawsuit regarding this incident. The chief academic officer said that the matter should be left alone, and was now behind them.

The student, on hearing about the decision, expressed her outrage to the CSAO. She did not want to go public with her accusation because of the publicity she might receive. However, she was extremely frustrated and angry at the university for not responding in any reasonable way to her charges.

In the next week, information about this matter was leaked by someone to the campus newspaper, and the article mentioned the name of the physics professor. This enraged the professor, the dean, and the chief academic officer. However, amid the professor's public objections, twelve other female students came forward and reported to the chief academic officer that they, too, had suffered sexual harassment from the same professor in the past three years. This, in turn, was reported in the newspaper, and an uproar was at hand. Over 300 students, both male and female, walked into the chief academic officer's office area and informed him that they intended to stay until he fired the physics professor and established a formal policy to handle sexual harassment complaints. This office occupation received statewide television coverage and infuriated the president and the board of trustees. After three days, the students finally left the building, due primarily to the efforts of the CSAO to negotiate with them (by now, she was the only administrator they trusted), and to assure them that the institution would establish a policy, that the professor's case would be fairly adjudicated, and that support would be provided to the affected students. A great deal of trust was lost on the part of the students, an individual student was treated very badly, the chief academic officer and deans became "enemies" of the students, the institution received negative publicity, and the president and the governing board became furious with the administrative staff's performance. What could the CSAO have done to help her institution avoid this very unfortunate conflict?

The student affairs leader had tried without success to convince the chief academic officer to adopt an adjudication process for resolving sexual harassment charges. Without such a process in place, the institution was very vulnerable to the problems that occurred. How could the CSAO have been more persuasive with the chief academic officer? Going to the president was not a good alternative, since he was not committed to the policy, and forcing such an administrative confrontation would so anger the chief academic officer that very little cooperation could take place in the future. The student affairs officer had introduced the issue at the administrative and deans council meetings, but that group had not responded positively to the idea. Two student organizations had been quite interested in seeing a sexual harassment policy established, and probably could have been prodded by the CSAO to approach the chief academic officer and the president. However, the student affairs leader has never used students to fight her battles and considers such tactics unethical. In retrospect, she believes she should have been more systematic in her attempts to persuade the chief academic officer. She might have considered the following strategies: (1) sharing written policies on sexual harassment from other well-known universities, (2) inviting the chief academic officer to a panel discussion on sexual harassment policies at a national higher education meeting, (3) sharing copies of actual court decisions regarding sexual harassment cases at other institutions, and (4) sponsoring a student affairs conference on this topic and asking a chief academic officer from another campus to be the keynote speaker. The CSAO might also have made the chief academic officer more familiar with the successful antiharassment policy she had established within student affairs to respond to student-to-student problems. Finally, she might have asked the university attorney to warn the chief academic officer that he and the institution might be subject to serious liability charges without a formal policy. Some of the approaches might have irritated the chief academic officer, but taken together they would have had a reasonable chance of causing the desired change.

The CSAO might also have helped her institution avoid the problems that occurred by involving key faculty members and academic deans in the mediation of conflicts among students. Where such involvement has occurred successfully, the faculty participants frequently become visible advocates for such procedures elsewhere. If they have had to adjudicate some student-to-student harassment cases, they might become convinced that a similar model could work well with the faculty.

Once the damage had taken place in this case, the CSAO was able to help mediate at least a temporary settlement, but the chief academic officer, the president, and the governing board had little choice but to "capitulate" to the student demands. The case illustrates how an institution can cause serious problems for itself by not adopting policies and procedures that allow conflicts to be resolved in a humane and orderly manner. It also suggests that CSAOs have an important role in urging all areas of the university to establish effective dispute settlement practices. While the incident described in this example did not occur within an area for which the CSAO had administrative jurisdiction, it did involve students, and the results were very negative for the entire institution. CSAOs have no corner on insight or monopoly on what is right, but they should work hard to persuade their colleagues that conflict resolution procedures should be established and should be well publicized and effectively implemented. Thus, an additional role of the CSAO as mediator is to make it possible for the process itself to occur in constructive ways throughout the institution.

The Effective Student Affairs Mediator: Suggestions for Good Practice

Student affairs administrators must be effective problem solvers if they are going to enjoy success. Conflicts among student groups and others are frequent occurrences, and the student affairs leader is expected to resolve them. Mediation skills are essential to accomplish these goals. Each campus is distinct, and CSAOs must adjust their problem-solving approaches to meet the special needs of their institutions. However, there are common mediation practices in student affairs that pertain to all campuses. Some suggestions for good practice in student affairs mediation are presented here.

Know the Students. It is difficult to imagine how conflicts among students could be resolved if the CSAO does not know the students well. There are no shortcuts to this essential task. Settling disputes requires trust, and trust is built over time by honesty, fairness, and personal contacts with students. When student groups clash over a hot campus issue, CSAOs do not just deal with the issue — as good mediators, they must know the students. Awareness of what the student group has done over the past few years, how it is perceived on campus, and who its leaders and members are are all very important to know. Often there are personal circumstances about individual students that CSAOs should be familiar with. There usually are key staff and faculty members who know the students well, and the student affairs leader should take full advantage of these contacts. If the student affairs officer has taken the time to get to know students and to earn their trust, then the task of mediating conflicts is much easier. If, however, the students only see the CSAO when there is a crisis or a conflict, they are not likely to respond favorably to his or her attempts to resolve the problem. CSAOs must spend a lot of their time "on the street," where students are, getting to know them as people. If they have done this well over time, then their attempts to resolve conflicts among these same students will seem a natural extension of their concern.

Understand the Issues. To stay well informed about the dozens of political, social, academic, and religious issues facing students is a very real challenge. This is especially true with the incredible cultural and ethnic diversity that exists on most campuses. CSAOs cannot, of course, be experts on the history of every group, but they must make concerted efforts to inform themselves about the fundamental issues that may be the source of campus conflicts. To be effective in mediating disputes, they may have to be knowledgeable about Chinese politics and history, the religious affiliation of Middle Eastern countries, constitutional issues regarding freedom of expression, or long-term rivalries and jealousies among social fraternities. They should read widely on these and other subjects and should listen to the students talk about them. They should also consult frequently with staff and faculty members who are experts in various fields. They should be close enough to the students to be able to anticipate conflicts before they arise. If a dispute erupts between two student groups and is reported on the front page of the newspaper, the president will hardly be pleased to learn that the CSAO knew nothing about it. It is impossible to overemphasize the importance of knowledgeability in the mediation process; this process is often extremely delicate, because angry people can become very sensitive about their beliefs and values. If student affairs leaders are not thoroughly familiar with the issues being disputed, their ignorance will quickly be exposed, and they will lose their credibility as mediators.

Develop Effective Skills. To be successful in resolving conflicts on campus, CSAOs do not simply call disputing groups together and wait for something magical to happen. They may think the prestige of their position or their own personal charisma will somehow convince others to drop their grievances. But a humbling yet necessary lesson especially for new CSAOs to learn is that their mere presence in a conflict will not result in an immediate solution. Worse, some student affairs administrators may think the way to resolve differences on their campuses is to call disputing groups together and order them to cease their actions. The nature of student life is far too complex for such approaches to work; the issues about which conflicts develop are often so volatile that naive or authoritarian efforts almost always fail.

Effective mediation skills are learned, and CSAOs must take the time to read the literature, attend conferences, and become familiar with good practices. There are often faculty members on the campus, usually in the business school, who are experts on the topic, and they can be sources of support and further education. Some student affairs staff have written case studies describing campus conflicts and used them to practice their mediation skills while being observed by critical advisers. CSAOs can explore possible techniques and strategies and find ways of applying them to various disputes. Representatives from one of the national mediation services could be invited to the campus as consultants, or the CSAO might choose to enroll in an educational program for developing mediation skills. Very few if any of the existing graduate preparation programs in student affairs and higher education include conflict resolution in their curricula, and as a result, CSAOs have had to learn these critical skills on their own. Successful problem solving requires more than a pleasant personality and sincerity; it requires a knowledge of the increasingly sophisticated area of mediation and an ability to apply its methods and techniques effectively.

Build Support with Teams. Successful mediation of conflict is rarely accomplished by one person, and when it works, several people almost always deserve the credit. Strong egos sometimes get in the way of efforts to resolve conflicts, and hard work is often needed to prevent this from happening. The CSAO is the key person in the mediation of student conflicts on the campus but is not necessarily the most visible participant in the actual process. One of the most effective ways to resolve conflicts is to build faculty-student mediation teams.

By carefully selecting and training small teams of faculty and student volunteers, the CSAO can create effective fits between certain issues and team skills. There may be one team particularly adept at addressing racial disputes, another at harassment, and another at residential disputes. Teams can increase the level of expertise, and can demonstrate a commitment on the part of the institution to a humane and participation-based method of solving problems. They may also be viewed as a neutral and unbiased way of resolving conflicts. They require extensive training, supervision, and evaluation, but they can greatly enhance the success of the campus mediation process if used correctly.

Earn the President's Support. The most successful student affairs mediators rarely involve their presidents directly in the resolution of campus disputes; they know their job is to earn their support by demonstrating effective problem-solving skills. With the backing of their presidents, they can proceed with confidence. On the other hand, if CSAOs are unsure of this support and are afraid they may lose their jobs if the conflicts are not resolved satisfactorily, they will not be effective mediators. They must be confident in their own ability to solve problems and persuasive with their presidents in convincing them that their approaches are sound. They should educate their presidents about the issues, make sure they understand the ways in which they intend to resolve conflicts, and make them aware that the process may take some time. They should be unambiguous about their approach to solving problems, because if the president is not clear about what is being done, confusion and anger can result when the outcomes are not pleasant.

The president's support is also important to the participants in campus disputes because they know the CSAO is speaking for the institution. This can send a crucial signal not only to the direct participants in the disputes but also to other members of the management team. In particular, the other vice presidents often have an interest in these conflicts and may grow impatient with the CSAO's approach. However, if they know the president strongly supports the mediation efforts of the student affairs leader, they will be much more likely to cooperate.

Confront the Unpleasant. Most administrators would like to see harmony among students, faculty, the community, and others. However, conflict is the norm. There are too many diverse backgrounds, too many competing interests, and too many strong convictions for it to be otherwise. It is this lively climate, however, that makes working in student affairs so stimulating and challenging. The best student affairs leaders are those who face conflict honestly and openly, recognizing that disputes are to be expected and that the existence of problems is not an indictment of them personally.

It is dangerous to deny that problems exist, in the hope that they will go away or solve themselves. When this is done, the problems inevitably get worse. Moreover, those affected wonder why no one has noticed what is wrong, or they resent the fact that no one has cared enough to do anything about it. Leaders do not earn the respect of others by sweeping problems under the rug; they do it by having the courage to confront real conflicts honestly and by trying to resolve them before they become unmanageable. This may lead some unpleasant problems to be exposed, causing embarrassment to individuals, groups, or the institution as a whole. But good education is not synonymous with the absence of conflict and embarrassment.

Use Mediation to Teach. Students often encounter problems with roommates, campus organizations, employers, or spouses and other family members. CSAOs are expected to solve these problems efficiently and fairly. If they are unable to accomplish this, they will probably be replaced. The best student affairs leaders accept this problem-solving role, but they also use the conflict mediating process as a way to teach students. By involving students in mediating their own problems, CSAOs help them learn to take responsibility for their own actions. When they see that a fair decision can be reached in difficult disputes by rational discussion and debate rather than by coercion, they have learned a valuable lesson. For example, several student groups may demand that the Asian-American Student Alliance not automatically be granted a seat in the student senate, causing a bitter dispute among student leaders on the campus. If the problem can be resolved humanely, in such a way that participants on both sides gain a greater respect for the rights of others, everyone will learn positively from the process. However, if a "solution" to the conflict is simply handed down in an authoritarian fashion, there will be winners and losers, and students may think the way to solve the problems is to find a powerful boss who will tell them what to do. In such cases, student affairs leaders must always keep their teaching role in mind, since their obligation to students' education is more important than any other responsibility they have.

Set an Example. CSAOs are very visible on their campuses. They are quoted almost daily in the student newspaper, and their presence is expected at countless student events. Even though most students may not be personally acquainted with them, they are well aware of their actions and public statements. The way CSAOs conduct themselves on a day-to-day basis with students, faculty, and staff therefore has a major impact on their ability to solve problems. If students see them as defensive, distant, and unconcerned, they certainly will not be able to settle student disputes. Their behavior as administrators must be interpreted as consistent from one situation to another. And CSAOs need to make sure that their daily actions and attitudes are consistent with the processes and goals used to resolve problems. Efforts to show compassion and concern when a crisis arises will be viewed with great skepticism if these same behaviors are not observed every day. In the way they treat students, involve them in decisions, listen to their ideas, and respect their backgrounds, student affairs leaders are "modeling the way" (Kouzes and Posner, 1987) and making it possible to solve problems later.

Learn to Compromise. A difficult lesson for many CSAOs to learn is that their solutions to campus problems will not always be adopted. They may, in fact, be right, but it is rare when everyone involved in a dispute accepts exactly the same solution. Stubbornness and rigidity are not compatible with successful mediation, and if student affairs leaders insist on getting their way all the time, they will encounter vigorous opposition and eventually failure. A reality of effective student affairs administration is that imperfect but workable compromises must be accepted if the campus is going to continue to function well. The very idea of mediation implies some form of compromise, and it should not be pursued if the CSAO has a predetermined solution to a problem and will not deviate from it, regardless of what others say or do. It is unethical for student affairs leaders to use the mediation process simply as a way to manipulate students. If the process is going to work, the participants must genuinely feel that they are, in fact, in charge of resolving the conflict, and that they have real choices available to them.

When CSAOs make a commitment to mediation as a way of settling disputes, they are expressing their confidence in the ability of the participants to develop a solution that will be acceptable to the institution. This clearly involves risk for the student affairs leader, and almost always means that a settlement will be reached that falls short of perfection. Most experienced CSAOs have learned that it is often better to accept small gains than it is to expect a total solution early in the process. Many conflicts are so complex (for example, racial relations) that no one decision is going to settle the issue. A common mistake made by new CSAOs is to assume that once a dispute has been settled, they can put it behind them, move on to something else, and not worry about it anymore. Students turn over rapidly, and many problems and disputes repeat themselves from one year to the next. Thus, problems do not just go away, which is another reason why learning to accept compromise is so necessary to successful student affairs administration.

Effective CSAOs must be skilled at mediating disputes and conflicts on their campuses. To carry out their most important responsibilities, they must also be educators. The next chapter presents a description of student affairs leaders as educators.

7

The Educator

Student affairs administrators can be good managers and problem solvers, but if they are not actively engaged in advancing the education of students, then they have abandoned their most important obligation as professionals. All of the programs and services in student affairs must support the educational mission of the institution. Student affairs leaders do not have to be inspiring teachers or seminar leaders to be effective in their role as educators, but they must be very good facilitators and organizers, persuading others to volunteer their skills and talents for the benefit of students.

In this chapter, I discuss issues and problems facing CSAOs in their role as educators. I include examples of how student affairs leaders can exert educational leadership on their campuses and offer suggestions for good practice.

Student Affairs as Education

Most students are only in classes or laboratories about 15–20 hours out of the 168 hours available in a week. Their out-of-class experiences can have a profound impact on their attitudes and values, their choice of academic majors and careers, their leadership ability, and their motivation for learning itself. While they rarely grant academic credit for extracurricular activities, most institutions encourage student participation in clubs, organizations, and service programs because they feel they have some value for student development. The early deans of student affairs were strong advocates of student participation in activities because they were convinced that involvement of this kind encouraged good citizenship and leadership. Their efforts, which were motivated by goodwill and idealism and were not based on any particular learning theory, were infrequently acknowledged by faculty members. Thus much of the early history of student affairs consisted of defensive efforts on the part of its practitioners to convince others (mainly the faculty) that their work had educational value. Ironically, the attempts of the early deans to fill the gaps in students' education caused by the retreat of the faculty into research may have reinforced the very separation they were reacting against. By recognizing and encouraging student activities, they were helping to legitimize aspects of the college experience that the colonial colleges had long sought to suppress or at least ignore. In many cases, this contributed to a dualistic notion of college, with the classroom being viewed as completely separate from student life. The chasm between academic pursuits and student life in higher education was the focus of three of the most influential books in the past decade (National Institute of Education, 1984; Boyer, 1987; Boyer, 1990), since most educators are now convinced that student involvement in programs and activities at their colleges contributes in substantial ways to their learning. There is also increasing awareness at many institutions that retention and graduation rates can be improved by getting students more personally engaged with their colleges.

    Student affairs leaders cannot just react to problems or provide services if they are to meet their obligations as educators. They must have strong convictions about what they want students to learn—both academically and in a broader sense—as a result of their college experiences. When candidates are being considered for the CSAO position, therefore, the most important criteria for selection should be the ability to articulate clear educational goals and a plan to achieve them. These objectives should be supported by the research literature (Newcomb, 1966; Feldman and Newcomb, 1969; Chickering, 1974; Astin, 1977; Withey, 1971; Kohlberg, 1981), and they should be appropriate to the institution. Most CSAOs are already familiar with the literature (for example, Chickering, 1969;

Schlossberg, Lynch, and Chickering, 1989) suggesting specific behavioral outcomes in students and ways to encourage and measure these efforts. Models are also available to assist colleges in formulating plans to encourage behavioral outcomes — such as increased racial awareness or improved speaking ability — and in evaluating them objectively. One of the key responsibilities of CSAOs is to use this available knowledge to the benefit of students' education by adapting it to the particular needs of the campus.

There are far too few student affairs staff members on most campuses to have a major impact on student attitudes and values on their own. Some student affairs leaders have tried to construct their own "curriculum," apart from the existing academic structure of the institution, to teach students certain skills and values. But such efforts almost always fail, because they affect so few students and because they are often viewed as quaint and isolated curiosities. Instead, collaboration and cooperation with the chief academic officer, academic deans, and the faculty are the keys to successful cocurricular programs in student affairs. This is particularly true because every college and university has faculty members with knowledge and skills that are essential to effective cocurricular programs. Tapping into this background of course requires the CSAO to be well acquainted with a large number of faculty members and to be able to convince them to participate in the planning and implementation of programs. Thus one of the key roles for the student affairs leader in developing strong educational experiences for students is that of a salesperson. In most institutions, faculty members do not earn credits toward tenure or promotion for their participation in student affairs cocurricular programs. CSAOs must understand this obstacle and find other ways to persuade good faculty to join them in attempts to educate students beyond the classroom. This requires competency and credibility on the part of the student affairs leader as well as the ability to demonstrate to faculty that their participation has benefits for students.

Students can and do learn in a variety of settings, and all students do not respond with equal enthusiasm to the same programs. The student affairs leader must be an expert on the learning styles and differences among students, and should be very sensitive to the ways in which special groups of students may react to cocurricular efforts. An off-campus retreat might be very effective in helping a sorority resolve some of its internal problems, but it might not work well for the Engineering Student Council. A series of invited speakers may not have as much impact on student behavior about AIDS as field trips to hospitals and urban care centers. New freshmen might learn more about values from a workshop at orientation than by simply being assigned to read a book about the topic. Certain residence halls may be much more receptive to a live-in faculty program than others. Some minority students may not be as familiar with study abroad opportunities as others, and thus should be targeted for this program. Many other examples could be presented to illustrate the need for student affairs leaders to recognize the differences among students and the ways various groups may respond to cocurricular programs. No campus, however small, has a homogeneous student body; it is the responsibility of the CSAO to study and understand the many smaller communities of students that it comprises and to plan a variety of programs to address their special needs.

It is a formidable challenge for student affairs leaders to stay focused on educational goals of this nature when they have to respond to so many problems and crises. In the interviews conducted as part of this study, many CSAOs reported that problem solving and crisis intervention could consume all their time and cause them to define their jobs only in these terms. Frustrated that they simply do not have sufficient time to pursue educational goals, some are leaving their positions. But many others thrive on the challenge.

Issues Facing the Student Affairs Educator

The following issues are important for CSAOs to consider as they plan and execute cocurricular programs for students.

The Role of Student Affairs. CSAOs must thoughtfully consider their role on the campus: Are they simply passive service providers, or are they active educators? How they decide this issue will affect how others view them, how effective their staff can be in educational programming, and what they can accomplish in cooperative efforts with the faculty. Because of their previous experiences, some administrators may not be accustomed to CSAOs who are actively engaged in the educational activity of the campus. They may think of student affairs as simply a set of support services, apart from the mainstream of the institution, existing only for the "care and feeding" of the students. This perception of student affairs is sometimes reinforced by CSAOs who do not view themselves as educators, or who remain on the academic sidelines of their campuses because they lack the credentials or the courage to participate. It is often easier for student affairs officers to retreat from educational and social issues, claiming that their only role is to admit students, disburse financial aid, and arrange for job placement interviews. But such an approach eliminates student affairs from the heartbeat of the campus and relegates it to a secondary, unexciting service role. Moreover, it is an abrogation of an important professional obligation of student affairs leaders regarding their educational responsibilities. The most successful student affairs leaders are convinced that the educational outcomes they seek for students are just as important as those sought in the traditional classroom setting, and are capable of articulating them clearly with faculty and students. They are frequent and enthusiastic participants in the academic life of the campus, raising questions about current priorities and making proposals of their own regarding new programs.

Involvement with the Faculty. Should the educational goals of student life be pursued in collaboration with faculty members or kept within the student affairs division? This question is frequently faced by CSAOs, whose staff members are usually interested in establishing leadership programs, health education seminars, cross-cultural workshops, and scores of other activities. Younger staff are especially tempted to organize such activities on their own, develop the strategy, and implement the efforts as "their program." Indeed, there is often such pride in ownership that others, including faculty and students, are kept out of the process entirely. Such isolated actions make planning quite easy, because the student affairs staff members are unfettered by outside ideas or different perspectives! But these efforts are also usually doomed to failure, since they have minimum visibility on the campus and no base of support from faculty. They can be problems for CSAOs as well if they become the "property" of certain staff, protected from scrutiny by others. Student affairs leaders want to encourage creative initiatives on the part of their staff, but they need to model the way for them, helping them avoid the isolation that will lead to failure.

Certain programs, such as stress management for residence hall students, campus recreation, and improving job interview skills can simply be done by student affairs staff members themselves. In other instances, however, such as dissertation anxiety sessions or academic majors exploration groups, the failure to involve the faculty in planning and implementation can result in hostility toward the student affairs staff. This is why teaching staff members how to collaborate successfully with the faculty in developing cocurricular programs is an especially important responsibility for CSAOs. Student affairs should be a collaborative enterprise, and CSAOs must provide the leadership to the staff in developing educational programs that reflect this principle.

Determination of Objectives. Most student affairs leaders are fortunate in that they have energetic and bright staff members who have dozens of good ideas for educational programs. Moreover, they work at institutions where their own contacts with faculty members result in many other ideas for improving educational experiences for students. A happy but difficult problem for CSAOs, then, is to decide — with the limited resources available — which ideas and programs to pursue. Should individual staff members be able to pursue their own priorities, or should some kind of centralized direction be given to them? What are the costs in creativity and enthusiasm if controls are placed on the staff? What if some staff members initiate programs on highly sensitive issues that end up embarrassing the college (and endangering the job of the CSAO)? These questions need to be addressed aggressively by the student affairs leader, so that educational programs can have their maximum impact and so that financial resources and staff talents can be used most efficiently. Because there are so many good ideas and so many issues to pursue, it is often advisable to create planning and coordinating committees to establish priorities and direction for a semester or an academic year. Some institutions have developed a broad educational theme for a year (such as international understanding) and have used this theme as a focus for much of their cocurricular programming. Student affairs officers should take the lead in these efforts.

Another pleasant problem faced by CSAOs in this area is how to get their own educational priorities implemented. In encouraging innovation by staff members, they are usually faced with so many good and creative ideas for programs that they have to work hard to get their own considered! They know that such programs are more likely to succeed if they emerge from within the staff, as opposed to being imposed from "above." As a result, often the best way for CSAOs to get their educational objectives implemented is by planting some informal seeds with staff in daily discussions with them. Proposals may then emerge that the student affairs leader considers essential to the needs of the campus.

Some CSAOs may have staff members who are quite eager to contribute but who are not well trained in program development. Without effective guidance and upgrading of skills, these individuals may experience frustration with unsuccessful programs, and the students will be shortchanged educationally. CSAOs must be sensitive to such problems, and should provide learning opportunities for staff members to develop needed skills. This is very important in efforts to maintain high-quality educational programs.

Academic Credit and Recognition. Students receive credits for their classroom work, and when they accumulate the right number and combination, a degree is awarded. Should they also be given academic credit for their service and leadership activities? Should student affairs leaders advocate such a position? Are academic credits or other forms of recognition needed to ensure the success of cocurricular programs? CSAOs have to address these questions in their efforts to develop educational activities.

Faculty often strongly resist the granting of academic credit for nonclassroom work, and many student affairs leaders themselves are skeptical of its benefits. They may feel that service and leadership should be their own reward, especially since one of the objectives is usually to instill a lifetime commitment to good citizenship behavior. However, others may feel that teaching six hours per week in a community literacy program deserves academic credit. If the decision is made to consider granting this credit for service and leadership activities, effective supervision by faculty and staff is mandatory. Clear definitions of acceptable cocurricular programs must also be developed. An effort should be made to see that these procedures are not too bureaucratic, since many student affairs leaders have found that the restrictions placed on credit-oriented activities are so cumbersome that they are not worth the trouble.

On the other hand, if credit is not given, other ways of recognizing the service and leadership accomplishments of students need to be found. The CSAO should make sure that the various means of doing this are fair and effective. Recognition programs must be genuine to be effective, and they present excellent opportunities to publicize the successful actions of students and the worth of the programs. Student affairs leaders should be especially sensitive to the need to recognize a wide variety of student activities, not just those that are most visible or politically acceptable. Recognition programs should also reflect the diversity of the student body in terms of age, gender, and ethnicity.

Relationship to General Education Goals. Most colleges and universities are currently engaged in lively debates about the purposes of undergraduate education and what, if anything, should constitute a common core of learning for all students. Such discussions are vital to the campus and inevitably raise important questions about desired educational and behavioral outcomes. Do student affairs leaders have contributions to make to these debates? Are such outcomes as international understanding or aesthetic awareness compatible with what student affairs staff members want to accomplish with students? Should the cocurricular efforts of student affairs leaders be patterned after the general education goals of the institution? CSAOs should thoughtfully consider these and related questions as they develop their educational strategy with their staff.

Student affairs leaders have a major responsibility to help close the gap between the classroom and campus life, and one way they can do this is to understand the general education goals of their institution and work to support them. Their relationship with the chief academic officer is very important in this regard, as it is with faculty members who are directly involved in teaching general education courses. If the formal academic program of the college is going in one direction and the activities of the student affairs staff are moving in another, then resources are being wasted and students will not learn as much as they can. The students must see connections between their classroom work and the "extracurriculum," or they will never experience any integration in their studies. They will tend to view their lives and the classroom as two separate entities, having little or nothing to do with each other. In collaborating with the faculty, student affairs leaders can provide experiential laboratories for students to apply the concepts they have learned in class. Such efforts can give new vitality to the learning process for students and can provide excellent opportunities for the student affairs staff to work closely with faculty members.

Social Engineering or Education? In planning educational programs and deciding on desired outcomes, student affairs leaders should be careful not to manipulate students' thinking into predetermined molds. Does a clear definition of an educational outcome imply a rigid orthodoxy or political position? Are cocurricular programs really designed to assist students in making independent judgments, or are they poorly disguised attempts at social engineering? Are programs pursued for their actual educational benefit, or are they really put in place to enhance retention, avoid crises, or generate favorable publicity? These are relevant ethical issues that CSAOs should face in planning and implementing educational programs. Students are not naive and will respond very negatively to programs they perceive as manipulative. Such efforts will backfire and will damage future programs. The purpose of cocurricular efforts can never be to get all students to think alike on some issue; ideas should be raised and experiences should be offered that enable them to formulate their own perspectives on issues. Indeed, cocurricular programs should be based on individual differences and freedom of choice. The college's role is not to impose certain values and attitudes, but to help students formulate their own views within a disciplined intellectual setting.

Evaluation Criteria. Educational programming in student affairs is a dynamic process that must be responsive to the needs of the students and the institution. It requires continual and sensitive evaluation, since some programs have to be discarded in favor of new ones. The CSAO should see that this evaluation process works well and that it is accepted by the various participating groups. Who should decide if cocurricular programs warrant continued support? What criteria should be used to evaluate their effectiveness? How much involvement, if any, should students have in the process? The CSAO should address these questions in formulating a coherent method of evaluating the educational activities of the division. There are always many more ideas and programs than the time and resources of the staff can accommodate. Moreover, each year new issues and problems need to be addressed. Some programs become entrenched after a few years, and it is very difficult to remove them. For example, most staff and faculty members might view the new-student orientation program as quite successful, but the new CSAO knows it is out of date and fails to include any substantive discussion of the college's educational goals. If an accepted way of regularly evaluating this program is not in place, it will be very difficult to change. Moreover, those most closely associated with its operation may be very resistant to assessment on any criteria except their own. For all these reasons, CSAOs need to develop ways to evaluate their cocurricular programs, including agreed-on criteria for evaluation. If done thoughtfully, evaluation can be an effective way to involve students, faculty, and staff in the process of building successful cocurricular programs. It can reinforce the need to focus on issues and outcomes related to the overall purposes of the institution and can encourage support for the effort by involving diverse groups in the process.

Student Affairs Education: Three Case Studies

To illustrate how CSAOs plan and implement cocurricular programs, the following examples are presented.

Student Volunteer Service Program. At this urban, selective, independent college of 1,500 students, faculty members have noted a marked increase in student preferences for careers that pay well. This is reflected in decreased enrollment in foreign language and humanities classes and a high demand for courses in computer science and business administration. This trend is viewed with considerable disdain by many faculty members, who think their students tend to be selfish, hedonistic, and interested only in using their academic degrees to advance their careers. Some of the student affairs staff share this cynical attitude and reminisce about the 1960s, when so many idealistic undergraduates at the college were joining the Peace Corps, helping people in the community, and pursuing social service careers. Student organizations used to volunteer their time at local agencies and schools, but most of this activity has disappeared. Now, they assert, most students spend their out-of-class time engaging in wild parties and could care less about social issues. Most faculty and student affairs staff members are skeptical of any effort to try to resurrect the volunteer spirit in the students, since they think the students' priorities are elsewhere.

The college has just hired a new CSAO from another institution, and the president has given her wide latitude in the programs and activities she might initiate. She is well aware of the situation on her new campus, having spent a good deal of time listening to students, faculty, and staff and observing the activities of students. Despite the cynicism and pessimism at the college, she is excited about the opportunities to introduce some change. She is convinced that there is a large reservoir of goodwill and idealism within the student body, and she intends to tap into it. How does she implement a successful student volunteer service program at her college?

She has a model clearly in mind, and she knows it can work because of her previous experience. However, being more committed to results than to a certain structure, she is willing to adapt her model to fit the needs of her current institution. Her primary task is to convince the chief academic officer, some key faculty, the student affairs staff, and a couple of visible student organizations that her plan is feasible and exciting. She has already made contacts with three community agencies that have very real needs for volunteer assistance: a literacy program for adults, a Big Brother–Big Sister program, and an after-school recreation program for children of single working parents. She wants the chief academic officer's support because faculty are needed as good supervisors of students' work, and they may be more inclined to get involved if the chief academic officer speaks in favor of the program. Student affairs staff need to be committed to the program to recruit students and to help convince them that their participation can make a difference. The two student organizations identified as good candidates to work in these initial programs need to be respected and visible. One of the first steps the CSAO takes is to ask the officers of the two groups to accompany her and some of the staff to the sites of the three programs needing assistance. She is convinced that when students have a chance to see and talk with the people and are introduced firsthand to their needs, they will respond positively. Her hopes are quickly confirmed, and the student leaders seem enthusiastic about the possibilities.

She knows these initial programs must be successful if her overall plan to involve most of the student body in volunteer service activities as an integral part of their academic programs is to be realized. Thus, she arranges for student training programs to be conducted by some of her staff, two faculty members, and a representative of each agency needing the service. She also recruits faculty volunteers, with the chief academic officer's help, to serve as the supervisors of the students working in the agencies. There will only be forty student volunteers in this initial effort, and she asked for one faculty member to supervise every ten students. After four weeks of training, the students are ready to begin their actual work. She knows that some will drop out, because they are impatient with slow progress or are overwhelmed by culture shock. But the training and frequent follow-up conferences with the supervisors have ensured that most students will stay with the project and will learn a great deal from involvement in it.

The CSAO knows that the key to expanding this program will be the actual experiences of the student volunteers. If they are enthusiastic about what they are doing, other students and student organizations will most likely want to get involved too. Thus, she spends considerable time with these student groups, making sure they know that she and her staff appreciate what they are doing and involving them in discussions about how to expand the program.

By planning a series of small wins, the CSAO succeeds in her efforts to increase student participation in the volunteer project within a three-year period. During this time, she has created a "student-faculty volunteer policy council," has jointly sponsored with the chief academic officer the first annual volunteer service conference for college students throughout the state, and has provided initial funding for a student publication on volunteer activities. She has succeeded in recruiting more faculty members as volunteers, and has established a new professional position on her staff to coordinate the program. She has organized an annual recognition program to thank outstanding volunteers for their work, and has been pleased to see five new student organizations formed to address specific service needs in the city. After only three years, she has succeeded in getting more than 50 percent of the students involved in volunteer service activities. She proceeded by asking some key people to work in programs that needed their help, rather than by preaching about the need for attitude changes. She knew if she could achieve some small successes with students and faculty, they would recognize the needs for further work on their own and would respond accordingly.

In this example, the CSAO had a clear educational goal in mind, a realistic strategy to accomplish it, and the patience and skill to implement it successfully. She focused her efforts on behavior change, not on attitude change, knowing that the former almost always precedes the latter. Despite the considerable obstacles facing her, she was able to develop this successful volunteer service program.

Racial Awareness Education. In this illustration, there has been considerable racial and ethnic unrest on a large Midwestern state university campus. There is a very diverse student body and growing resentment among many white students about what they perceive as preferential treatment for minorities. Racial slurs have been written on bulletin boards, and ethnic groups have expressed fear for their safety. A large amount of negative publicity throughout the state about this racial turmoil has made the university president very uneasy, and legislators, alumni, parents, and others are suggesting publicly that various actions should be taken to address the problem. The admissions office reports that applications for the next fall's freshman class are down by almost 20 percent, and high school counselors are saying that the university's reputation as a cold and insensitive institution is to blame. The CSAO has worked hard to avoid these problems but with limited success. He was able to convince a reluctant president to appoint a special faculty-student committee on racial tensions, and he has been meeting with this group for several weeks. It is hoped that recommendations will emerge from this committee that will have sufficient substance and credibility to gain the support of the institution's academic and administrative leadership. After four months of intensive and often bitter debate, the major recommendation of the special committee is to require all undergraduate students to enroll in a newly established three-credit course to be called "American Racial and Ethnic Relations." This recommendation is enthusiastically endorsed by the student government association and all of the ethnically based student organizations. However, it is quickly rejected by the faculty senate, which argues that the recommendation is unwieldy and impossible to implement. The senate also objects to the suggestion that the purpose of academic instruction is to impose any particular point of view on students. This refusal of the faculty senate to respond favorably to the recommendation of the student-faculty committee only serves to exacerbate racial tensions. It also causes concerned students to become more skeptical about the commitment of their university to multicultural education.

The CSAO was responsible for getting the committee on racial awareness appointed, and supports its recommendation for the course. The faculty senate is a very influential body, and its actions are almost always accepted by the president. Moreover, the president knows that to order the faculty to teach something they have not initiated themselves simply will not work. The student affairs leader feels an urgent sense of responsibility in this situation to help initiate some educational experiences for students. What should he do?

The chief academic officer is also uneasy, and she and the CSAO have remained in close contact through all of the committee's deliberations and the faculty senate's discussion. They know it is unrealistic to force the faculty to teach a course for all students, but they also know that something must be done and that the president expects them to get it done. The spring semester will end in five weeks, and the summer term is a relatively quiet time, when some planning might be done. They know they need to have something in place by the beginning of the fall semester. The CSAO suggests that twenty-five key faculty members be recruited as volunteers to develop special courses on race relations for the fall semester. The faculty could come from a variety of disciplines, and no prescription as to content would be given. The courses could be taught under a "special topics" arrangement in each department for one year, since a faculty senate regulation allows such experimental courses. The CSAO also suggests that a special registration sign up for these courses be made available late this spring as well as for the summer freshman orientation. He includes a list of eight well-respected student affairs staff members who are willing to teach the course, and offers the residence hall multipurpose rooms as additional space for teaching some of the sections. Finally, he suggests that he and the chief academic officer personally invite specific faculty to teach the class, and that they jointly ask the president for an allocation of $150,000 from the university foundation to fund it. The CSAO is very concerned about the volatile nature of the issue, and knows the institution needs to take some solid, visible action very soon. Thus, he and the chief academic officer go immediately to the president with the proposal.

The president concurs and asks them to proceed as quickly as possible, because he is confident he can secure the needed financial support. He suggests inviting some graduate students to assist the regular teacher, and urges both the chief academic officer and the CSAO to teach one of the courses themselves. They think this is an exciting idea, since neither of them has taught undergraduates for several years. They also hope that their willingness to teach might send an important signal to the rest of the faculty.

The chief academic officer and the CSAO then call a meeting of major student organization leaders, the student government, and the campus newspaper staff to announce the plan of action. Before the meeting, they had secured commitments from fifteen faculty members who agreed to teach classes in history, English, anthropology, political science, marketing, education, and other fields related to race relations. While the students were disappointed that their original proposal for a required course for all students would not be implemented, they were pleased that the university was responding in some way to their request for multicultural education.

More than 500 students registered for the various courses, and the response in the fall semester from faculty and students was so positive that the faculty senate itself appointed a committee to recommend further course development in every academic department. The racial tensions on campus have not disappeared, but the CSAO and the chief academic officer feel that the relatively small educational program they were able to put in place has had positive outcomes. They understood the need, knew the students, and decided that something had to be done despite the original rejection of the course approval by the faculty senate. The CSAO was effective in improving the academic program by working closely with the chief academic officer and contributing his staff resources, facilities, and expertise.

Student Leadership Development. At this private university of 10,000 students, there is a great deal of tradition in student government and student organizations. The social fraternities have controlled student leadership positions in the major campus groups for decades, since their political and social influence has been very strong. There are leadership honoraries for sophomores, juniors, and seniors, and membership in these groups has also been controlled by the fraternities. Women, minorities, and members of academic and service groups have had very few campuswide leadership options, because they have been effectively shut out of them by a tightly controlled political system they deeply resent. There have been a few attempts to reform this situation in past years, but the fraternities have successfully blocked them. While faculty at the university are not very involved in student life, they are aware of the dominance of the fraternities, and as a result, most of them view "student leadership" on the campus with cynicism and disdain. The students who have the power annually congratulate themselves for having what they claim is the "best student government in the country," but they choose not to participate in state or regional student leadership conferences because they feel they are so far ahead of their peers.

The CSAO, who just retired, had been on the campus for many years and was part of this system himself. The newly appointed student affairs leader came from another institution, but she has studied the situation and understands it very well. In her first week on the job, she is visited by a delegation of fraternity leaders, who explain to her how things work in student life at this university and how she should conduct her office. She is also visited by a number of other students, who see her appointment as a chance to reform the system. She listens politely to all of them without indicating any preference for any particular actions. Most of her staff are fed up with the dominance of the fraternities in student life and have given up trying to change the situation. They simply have decided to spend their time elsewhere, with other student groups.

The CSAO knows that the quality of student leadership is low, that many of the students seem to be more interested in maintaining what they think is power than in providing service, and that many other students are frustrated by the system itself. She has discussed the situation with the chief academic officer and the president to get their views, and learns that they are not at all concerned about it. "That's just student politics; it's always been that way; just leave it alone," they suggest. She has no intention of leaving it alone, and knows she faces a tough challenge in changing long-standing student traditions and indifferent faculty attitudes. She is convinced that this situation is not conducive to a healthy campus climate, and knows that education is the only answer. How does she proceed?

She has no intention of choosing sides, and she has no desire to alienate the fraternities. In fact, she knows that she needs their support, and she genuinely wants to improve the quality of leadership on the campus for all students. During her first semester, she visits all of the fraternities and many other student organizations as well, making sure she is well known by them. Everywhere she talks about student leadership, and she generates considerable interest in the topic by introducing students to new leadership concepts. She also gets to know some key faculty members in business, law, education, and political science who have been teaching courses on various aspects of leadership for years. She convinces five of her own staff members to attend professional development conferences on leadership, and gradually convinces the chief academic officer that teaching leadership to undergraduates is a good idea. She also has spent time with the development vice president, who has assisted her in contacting foundations and corporations for financial support. She intends to eventually establish a "student leadership institute," funded primarily with private dollars.

Building on the credibility she has established with student organization officers, she forms a student-faculty leadership committee to plan a series of events for new students for the beginning of the next academic year. She suggests to the committee that a campuswide leadership conference might be planned and implemented. Such an event has never been held on the campus, and if the president, the chair of the board of trustees, and some challenging speakers could be attracted to it, the impact could be very positive. Thanks to the enthuasiastic assistance of her own staff, the conference is held and is very successful. Now the CSAO feels the time is right to advance her proposal for the leadership institute.

She proposes a three-tiered, two-year-long "curriculum" of noncredit courses on leadership taught by student affairs staff and college faculty. Some 250 students would be selected for participation in the program during the first year by a staff-faculty committee. Students would do extensive reading, participate in dispute settlement exercises, learn effective communication skills, discuss case studies, and visit other university and corporate leadership settings. At the end of each semester-long course, those who successfully completed the requirements would receive certificates at a public ceremony sponsored by the student affairs division. The CSAO is able to secure financial support for the leadership institute from corporations, which also contribute the time of some of their managers who agree to teach in the program.

Students accept the program with great enthusiasm, and requests to participate in it far outnumber available spaces. The CSAO was skillful enough to present it to the campus only after several months of groundwork had been laid, and without any political agenda in mind. By focusing on positive learning outcomes and the participation of a diversity of students, the program has excellent potential to increase the quality of life on the campus. In the process, it is also very likely that some of the negative traditions and provincialism will be eroded and will be replaced by more enlightened approaches to leadership. Most important, an educational program has been put in place that can teach valuable skills to students, and its potential for growth is very promising. Moreover, as the CSAO delights in reminding her president, the leadership institute is funded entirely by private dollars.

The Effective Student Affairs Educator: Suggestions for Good Practice

This section provides suggestions for good practice regarding the educational role of the chief student affairs officer.

Understand Student Cultures. To achieve success in student affairs educational programs, it is essential to know the students, as well as the many smaller communities that are part of the student body. Thus student affairs leaders must study their students, both formally and informally, to identify and understand their preferences, concerns, and cultural backgrounds. A regular assessment program should be in place, but student affairs administrators should also "walk the streets" frequently to learn on a firsthand basis how students live and what their concerns are. Students are so diverse on most campuses that educational programs sponsored by student affairs staff must be targeted to special groups to be effective. Instructional methods may have to be adapted to fit the learning styles of these groups, and to accomplish educational goals, CSAOs should work to build a variety of talents on the part of staff members.

Know the Direction. Student affairs administrators should be thoughtful educators themselves—experts on student culture, learning styles, and higher education. Before they assume their positions, they should have strong and passionately felt ideas of what they want to accomplish in terms of student learning. The principal reason to hire a specific CSAO should be his or her ability to articulate and implement an effective educational program for the campus. This does not mean student affairs leaders should have some rigid plan that they impose on the campus but they do need to have a clear idea of what students can learn in cocurricular programs that fit the distinctive nature of each institution. CSAOs need to provide the leadership to the rest of the staff by convincing them that the desired outcomes are achievable and worthwhile. They also must be able to earn the support of students in developing and implementing educational programs. A key to accomplishing these goals is to know clearly what objectives are being pursued.

Sell, Persuade, and Promote. CSAOs are enablers and facilitators for others. It is their job to make things happen. If cocurricular programs are to be successful, and if faculty, staff, and students are to become active supporters, most of the responsibility will be the student affairs leader's. One of the major reasons for the failure of some CSAOs is their inability to sell, persuade, and promote their ideas. Sometimes the problem is excessive use of psychological jargon that confuses and frustrates people, and other times it may be inadequate planning or ineffective interpersonal skills on the part of the student affairs leader. Ideas do not sell themselves, and considerable efforts are needed to convince others that educational programs are worthy of their support and participation. Frustrated with the lack of response by faculty members and others outside the division, some student affairs leaders retreat into a corner of the campus and attempt to conduct educational programs on their own. This is "preaching to the choir," and it eventually results in antagonism from faculty and isolation from the mainstream of student life. This responsibility to sell and promote does not mean that CSAOs must be charismatic entrepreneurs; it does suggest that they be credible, visible, hard-working spokespersons for their divisions. They must understand and accept the fact that what their staff can accomplish in cocurricular programs depends to a great extent on their ability to convince others of its worth.

Collaborate and Build Teams. As with management and mediation functions, student affairs leaders must be effective collaborators and team builders if they are to achieve success in their role as educators. The best way to build support for cocurricular programs is to develop cooperative relations with faculty and students. Student affairs administrators can provide the initial leadership, but the development and implementation of programs should be done by teams of faculty, staff, and students. CSAOs must encourage their staff to involve others in programs, even though it may make the process longer and more complicated. Student affairs educational programs cannot exist for long in isolation from the faculty, and the best way to ensure their success is through collaboration. AIDS education, multicultural programs, and leadership seminars will all be stronger if they involve the most talented faculty members on the campus. Moreover, they will have more visibility, and will demonstrate to students that a broad range of professionals at the institution support them.

Many student affairs staff members have excellent backgrounds in assessment, program development, evaluation, and student cultures. As a result, they may join faculty colleagues in writing grant proposals for specific educational projects. Such activity provides an ideal opportunity for collaboration and cooperation. Student affairs–faculty teams find support for their proposals in such areas as career exploration, retention, and volunteer service education. CSAOs should encourage such activity by suggesting possible funding sources, describing needed programs, and identifying faculty likely to participate.

Some student affairs leaders often formalize the collaboration process by appointing several committees of faculty, staff, and students to develop a variety of cocurricular programs. Groups can have responsibility for orientation, leadership, intergroup relations, international education, and many other issues and activities. This approach may ensure that faculty, staff, and students will be involved in cocurricular programs, but CSAOs should work to see that such groups do not become static over a period of time.

Work with the Chief Academic Officer. The chief academic officer is responsible for all teaching and research programs. He or she has control of most of the budget, is very influential with the deans and department chairs, and is a very visible person on campus. Thus the student affairs leader needs to develop a very close and trusting relationship with the chief academic officer if he or she is serious about contributing to educational goals. It may take some time, but the CSAO must persuade this official that the various activities and programs in student affairs are important aspects of the institution's educational program. This is best accomplished by conducting successful activities in cooperation with faculty and by making sure the chief academic officer is actively involved in them. A prerequisite, of course, is that the student affairs leaders be very familiar with the general education program of the institution and be ready to make substantive suggestions and contributions toward its improvement. It is also essential to understand other major curriculum programs on the campus, both undergraduate and graduate, and to be able to provide helpful support to them.

Seek and Secure Resources. Most CSAOs have the happy situation of working with highly talented, energetic, and creative staff who have lots of exciting educational ideas. One of their major challenges is to find the resources that will enable their staff to carry out their programs. Indeed, many staff feel the major function of the CSAO is to find the money, personnel, and space that will enable them to do their jobs. Very few, if any, colleges and universities have sufficient resources to meet all the needs identified by student affairs personnel. This, of course, means that CSAOs must seek other sources for support beside those within the institution's budget. User fees, tuition add-ons, foundation and corporation grants, alumni and parent donations, and state and federal agency support are only a few of the options currently being pursued by student affairs leaders. Cooperation with the chief development officer is also advisable, and some CSAOs now have full-time professional fund raisers on their own staffs to secure additional resources.

There are many good ideas for educational programs in student affairs, but almost all of them cost money. It is not enough for student affairs leaders to be knowledgeable about academic issues; they have to be successful in finding resources to support their programs. Otherwise, the morale of the staff will suffer, creativity will diminish, and very little meaningful education will take place. It is unrealistic for student affairs leaders to expect their institutions to provide them with all the resources they need; it is their responsibility to secure them through their own initiatives.

Evaluate the Programs. Most evaluation of cocurricular activities in student affairs is either informal or consists of simple reactions from participants at the end of an event. Such efforts certainly have value, but they do not contribute to substantial or long-term understanding of student learning. If CSAOs are serious about the outcomes they are seeking to encourage through their programs, then a systematic and largely independent method of evaluation should be put in place. In many cases, staff directly involved in planning and conducting cocurricular programs are too attached to them to be unbiased observers of their effectiveness.

On most campuses, there are faculty experts who can assist in setting up evaluation programs for student affairs educational activities. Many student affairs staffs also have persons with excellent skills in this area.

Some CSAOs invite external review teams to their campuses on a periodic basis to evaluate specific educational programs. This can be a time-consuming and expensive process, but also one that can yield information and insights that cannot be gained in any other way. Those not directly associated with a campus can often see problems that are unnoticed by those who are directly connected with them.

A rigorous evaluation program can improve quality, provide guidance for planning, and enhance the acceptance of programs on the campus as a whole. It is the responsibility of the CSAO to put this evaluation program in place.

Set an Example. The primary function of CSAOs is education. In all of their activities, no matter how difficult and stressful, they must always keep uppermost in their minds how their actions and decisions might affect the education and growth of students. This is the example they must set for their staff, and the standard they should adopt for their work. If they are doing their jobs well, student affairs leaders are very visible and well known at their institutions. They should make their educational goals, standards, and priorities clear to students and share their beliefs with them. How they talk with students, how they handle conflicts, and how they respect the views of students may send stronger educational messages than the content of the programs themselves. At a retreat on racial awareness, for example, the way students view the actions of student affairs leaders is more important than any speeches they make. This is not to suggest that CSAOs need to be above reproach. On the contrary, the more like very ordinary human beings they act, the more likely they are to have a positive influence on students' education.

Part Three

Professional Concerns and Commitments

8

Assessing
and Developing
Professional
Effectiveness

Student affairs administrators are responsible for a very diverse array of programs and services, and face different expectations from students, faculty, parents, the community, the governing board, and their presidents. Within this complex campus environment, how should the professional effectiveness of CSAOs be evaluated? What criteria should be applied, who should decide on the criteria, and how should the performance of CSAOs be monitored? What professional development activities are desirable to enhance the effectiveness of student affairs leaders? In view of the changing nature of the position and the often unpredictable demands placed on CSAOs, what educational backgrounds or career paths may provide the best foundations for future leaders in student affairs? These are the issues addressed in this chapter.

Evaluating Performance

Because of the nature of the position, those who become CSAOs are usually very strong willed and confident persons. Nevertheless, they have the same needs as others to know how they are doing in the job and whether their performance is meeting the

179

expectations others have of them. They also have a very strong interest, of course, in how they will be evaluated, and in what the evaluation of criteria will be. There are several factors that make it difficult to reach agreement on the criteria used to evaluate CSAOs.

Presidential Priorities. One president may believe that a calm and harmonious campus is the most important objective for student affairs, and another may believe that dramatic improvement in service efficiency to students is most important. Other priorities can emphasize facilities development, enrollment enhancement, or the resolution of difficult social issues. Since chief executive officers turn over fairly quickly, CSAOs must be very responsive to the particular priorities of their presidents and aware that what they might have done quite well in the past may not be valued by their new bosses. This can cause confusion and frustration for student affairs leaders, especially if their own priorities for their work do not match the expectations of the president. This situation clearly demands flexibility on the part of CSAOs, and a recognition that there are no fixed, absolute evaluative criteria that can be applied to their performance. It also suggests that CSAOs should be very candid about these matters when they are appointed and when new presidents are named. Presidents deserve to have administrators who can carry out their priorities, and if CSAOs are not comfortable with them, it is their obligation to inform their presidents of this and probably to seek another position.

Institutional Problems. Major priorities for colleges and universities change, and not all CSAOs can be effective in addressing these priorities equally well. During the 1960s, CSAOs were often expected to be effective crisis managers because of student political turmoil; in the 1990s, they may be expected to be good financial administrators, facilities managers, or fund raisers. The skills required are very different, and CSAOs working today cannot expect to be evaluated by criteria that were relevant only to an earlier time. The skills of student affairs leaders should match the needs of their institutions, and this, of course, has a major impact on the criteria used to evaluate them.

Vulnerability of the Position. CSAOs do not produce student credit hours, administer degree-granting academic programs, or earn money for their institutions. They function in the broad arena of student life, which invites almost everyone to offer an opinion as to what should be done! There is no measurable, universally accepted standard as to what student life should be like, and thus CSAOs are always vulnerable to the wishes and priorities of others over whom they have no control. If parents are upset about poor security on the campus, the CSAO may make a very convenient scapegoat and may be dismissed if the issue becomes highly visible. While there are many constituent groups for the CSAO, there is no external professional support group, in the way that a bar association may support the dean of the law school. The primary role of professional student affairs associations is to encourage the development and education of their members, not to intervene in institutional matters.

To summarize, the CSAO is vulnerable because of the nature of the position, the fluid character of student life, and the lack of any clearly defined support group. It is very unlikely that this situation will change, and it poses major difficulties in establishing clear evaluative criteria for the position.

Single-Issue Evaluation. In the interviews conducted as part of this study, several CSAOs mentioned their fear of becoming victims of a single issue on their campuses that could place them in jeopardy. They could be effective financial managers and excellent service providers, but if a gang rape occurred in a fraternity, or a racial incident took place in a residence hall, their performance and effectiveness could be called into question. Various constituencies might view the single incident as sufficient evidence to remove the CSAO from office, and if the heat gets turned high enough, even a supportive and understanding president may not be able to resist it. The unfairness of such situations cannot be changed by CSAOs; they must simply learn to accept this as part of their positions. However, single-issue problems also confound efforts to establish clear evaluative criteria for the CSAO's performance.

Popularity. The student affairs field does not have outcomes that are easily recognized and measured. It is a "people business," and the way in which the CSAO is perceived as a person influences its effectiveness. To ignore this reality in the evaluation of CSAOs is to overlook a very significant factor. Everyone in the field is aware of the impact popularity (or lack of it) can have. Even though their leadership has not produced anything tangible in the way of policies, programs, or facilities, some CSAOs seem to survive for a while simply because they are popular members of the campus community. Those who are less well liked often have the opposite experience — encountering a frustrating lack of acknowledgment or appreciation even for major achievements. What this underscores, of course, is that student affairs leaders are very public persons on their campuses and in their communities, and whether they like it or not, their personalities inevitably affect what others think of them. This is not to suggest that CSAOs must manipulate others to gain popularity; it does mean that they must be sensitive to their public image, because it affects the way others evaluate their work.

Resource Availability. Another difficulty in establishing fair evaluative criteria for student affairs administrators is the availability of resources. Most experienced CSAOs are very familiar with this problem. Their requests for additional staff resources and additional computer support in student financial aid may have been ignored for a period of years, yet when students, parents, and auditors complain loudly and publicly about poor service delivery from that office, CSAOs are held accountable! Their performance is evaluated as very poor, because the job did not get done. It may result in the dismissal of the CSAO and the appointment of a new student affairs leader — who is then granted the necessary resources to improve financial aid delivery. It is very difficult to establish objective criteria for the evaluation of CSAOs that adequately address such problems.

It is a reality of the position, and if the student affairs leader and the president do not have a trusting relationship, misunderstanding and frustration will result. Moreover, the CSAO is very likely to feel bitter about the unfairness of the evaluation.

Skepticism. As Kerr (1980, p. 423) suggests, many faculty members and administrators are skeptical of impressionistic or informal evidence that seems to involve more value judgments than actual data. Munitz (1980, p. 480) confirms this by pointing out that many senior administrators in organizations are very doubtful that any fair or objective criteria can be applied to their work. The absence of any accepted objective criteria may make some CSAOs feel that the informal evaluations they receive do little but cause them additional anxiety. Moreover, some fear that the evaluation process will be used to manipulate them into accomplishing the personal or institutional goals of others. And some CSAOs may object that the evaluation criteria are not relevant or useful enough to contribute to their own growth and development. Many presidents are also skeptical about the evaluation process. This is partly because they understand the great complexity of the issues involved; in addition, they may want to avoid the sometimes unpleasant task of confronting personnel problems that add to their already overtaxed agendas.

Who Should Determine the Criteria?

Student affairs administrators are well known on campus and so their effectiveness is usually judged by many groups, not all of whom may agree on either the criteria or the performance. The following individuals and constituencies should have a role in the evaluation process.

The President. CSAOs are hired by presidents and are responsible to them. The primary duty for deciding the criteria for evaluation of the student affairs leader rests with the president. CSAOs must have the confidence of knowing that they are conducting their offices in accordance with the president's priorities, and that these administrators will support their actions. If their presidents expect them to increase the enrollment and balance the budget in the residence halls, then they had better not spend most of their time trying to upgrade the counseling program! They deserve to know from their presidents what it is they are expected to do, how much time they have to do it, and what resources will be available to them. They also need to have the understanding and support of their presidents before single-issue problems and crises occur. They must help their presidents learn that various groups have strong agendas of their own that may conflict with those of the CSAO. Student affairs leaders cannot expect the unqualified support of their presidents all the time; the issues are often too complex for this to be the case. What they should expect is an honest, forthright agreement at the time of appointment that spells out what is expected of them and how and when they will be evaluated. Most presidents do not claim to be experts in student affairs, and are quite open to suggestions and guidance from their CSAOs as to how the evaluation should be done. The key is to be as explicit about the process as possible, because to ignore it or to assume that the president's understanding matches the CSAO's may be a serious error.

Students, Faculty, and the Community. While none of these groups has the authority to decide how CSAOs will be evaluated, each has a very significant influence on their success. Student affairs leaders should never take the support of these groups for granted. They should nurture their relationships with them, and invite their feedback on their performance. Many experienced CSAOs seek such evaluative information from student, faculty, and community groups on a regular basis, and share it with their presidents and with their staff. This approach encourages trusting relations with these important groups, and also avoids placing student affairs administrators in a defensive or reactive posture with them. Such an approach not only may engender support for CSAOs, it may also enable them to introduce these groups to ways of looking at student affairs they had not considered before.

The Other Vice Presidents. CSAOs are members of the institutional management team, and must cooperate with the other vice presidents in making major policy decisions. However, they also compete directly with the other vice presidents for resources and for the president's support for their own programs. Sometimes this competition can become very vigorous, and bad feelings can develop among the vice presidents as a result. CSAOs must be very sensitive to these relationships, because the other vice presidents evaluate their performance every day. Even though CSAOs do not report to anyone but the president, it is very difficult to maintain the president's support if the academic and financial vice presidents view their performance with disdain. CSAOs can avoid some problems that can affect how they are evaluated by sharing their concerns with these colleagues and showing sensitivity to their needs. This process can strengthen the team concept, and improve the effectiveness of the evaluation procedure by encouraging each vice president to learn more about the other team members.

The Student Affairs Staff. The most rigorous evaluation of CSAOs almost always comes from the staff itself. Staff members are the most knowledgeable, see the student affairs leader every day, and are in the best position to understand how policies and programs are actually received. It may be possible for some of the other groups mentioned earlier to misjudge the effectiveness of CSAOs for a time, but it is rare for the student affairs staff to be off target. Experienced student affairs leaders know this very well, and while they report formally only to the president, they know they must earn the respect and support of their staff every day. The staff does not formally decide how CSAOs will be evaluated, but if they have a low opinion of their performance, then these administrators can achieve little success.

It does not do student affairs leaders much good to hear from their staff that they are well liked, although it may be pleasing to know this. What they need to know is how effectively they are perceived as leaders in helping the institution reach its objectives in student life. Asking for these kinds of evaluative comments can be threatening, because the results may surprise and dishearten the student affairs leader. However, to avoid doing so, or merely to assume that there is support for one's performance, can create worse problems. The best CSAOs know that they can benefit from evaluation by their staff, and that the process can enhance trust and affirm the professional nature of staff relations.

A Personal Decision. As Canon (1980, p. 440) suggests, some student affairs administrators may feel it is their own responsibility to decide how they will be evaluated, because only they can know how they are really doing. They may readily admit that they must answer to the president and be very responsive to numerous groups and individual expectations. However, they may argue that they have some internal gut feeling that should supersede any other form of evaluation. They may insist that they will instinctively know when their performance as leaders is no longer appreciated, and will voluntarily step aside at that time. But while such insight is enviable, very few CSAOs possess it. Moreover, such an internalized approach to evaluation may mask a fear of opening up one's performance to others, or simply a professional snobbishness that only a "select few" can know the truth. It may engender resentment among staff and other colleagues as well, if CSAOs give the impression that they have appointed themselves to a status not available to others. Evaluation of professional effectiveness cannot exist in isolation from one's colleagues, and should be as explicit and as objective as possible. High standards for personal performance are laudable, but no senior administrator should be exempt from rigorous evaluation in relation to clearly stated objectives.

What Criteria Should Be Used?

Institutional leaders can establish many criteria for the evaluation of the professional effectiveness of CSAOs. The following represent the major options.

Student Education and Growth. Evaluating the effectiveness of CSAOs on the basis of student growth and development poses similar difficulties to assessing professors on the basis of their teaching. It is clearly the most important criterion, but it is extremely difficult to describe objectively because the specific conditions that lead to student learning are elusive at best. One of the greatest satisfactions in student affairs is to observe the personal growth of students while they are in college — improved self-confidence, enhanced leadership skills, greater cultural sensitivity, or a stronger sense of service to others. But students may demonstrate such growth as a result of many experiences, some associated with their college education and some not. The existence of certain programs and interventions does not automatically lead to precise outcomes. And though it is possible to obtain good measures of changes that occur in students' attitudes and values and in their satisfaction with their studies during their college years, it is very difficult to assign "credit" for these changes to one administrator. These difficulties result in frustration for student affairs professionals, who find themselves evaluated on other less elusive criteria, ones they feel are not the most important measures of their work. CSAOs should work closely with their presidents to reach an understanding of how student growth and development will be assessed as part of the evaluation of the student affairs leader.

Management Efficiency. Many CSAOs reported in the interviews conducted as a part of this study that they were most often judged on the basis of their ability to deliver services in an efficient manner. This evaluative criterion includes sound fiscal management, and especially in state universities, the absence of unfavorable audits. It increasingly involves effective management of campus facilities. CSAOs accept management efficiency as an important measure of their work, and recognize that they will be held accountable for delivering services and handling money. Most, however, reject it as the most important or sole criterion for the evaluation of their efforts. It is possible to be efficient financially while not addressing the most important social problems or educational issues of students. CSAOs must perform well in this area, but should not delude themselves into thinking that favorable evaluations as efficient managers mean that they have achieved real success.

Problem Solving. Problem solving is accepted by CSAOs as an important evaluative criterion for their work. Of course, they are not expected to be miracle workers, able to settle every dispute that occurs; however, they are expected to take charge and achieve positive results most of the time. If they are indecisive, or take every problem to the president to resolve, most people will lose confidence in them as leaders.

Problem-solving ability as an evaluative criterion for the CSAO must be considered in relation to the educational goals of the campus and the priorities of the president, since these can vary. On campuses where social turmoil is viewed negatively, problem solving can become the dominant measure of performance. Fearful of receiving unfavorable evaluations, some CSAOs may try to keep the campus as quiet as possible, avoiding discussions of volatile issues and discouraging student groups from engaging in political activities. If the campus is peaceful, the CSAO must be doing a good job, according to this criterion. But this strategy may not be as highly regarded on other campuses.

Campus Climate. As the administrators responsible for giving direction to student life, CSAOs are very concerned with the institutional climate or the health of the campus. When the stress level is very high, it will be reflected in student behavioral problems, including vandalism, substance abuse, and suicide. If CSAOs are not strong and sensitive leaders in addressing the health of the campus, they will be viewed as ineffective. This is an evaluative criterion that is probably impossible to quantify, but presidents understandably expect CSAOs to take positive actions regarding the campus climate. A 50 percent reduction in suicide attempts or a 25 percent reduction in violent crime may not signify a greatly improved campus climate, since other, less obvious signs of stress and disharmony may be increasing; but CSAOs are increasingly aware that such statistics affect the way they are evaluated. As a result, most student affairs leaders have become very aggressive in their efforts to enhance the campus climate, not just for the benefit of students but also because they know they will be partially judged on its overall health.

Sensitivity and Concern. Student affairs administration is not just a mechanical process of managing services and solving problems; CSAOs are expected to demonstrate sensitivity and concern in all they do. The campus community reacts very unfavorably to student affairs leaders who do not show compassion for students and their problems. The president will receive lots of feedback about such behavior if it occurs, and nothing can damage the effectiveness of CSAOs more than insensitive or uncaring treatment of students. This performance expectation for CSAOs rarely appears in any letter of appointment or job contract, but it is a very important criterion for evaluation. The failure to display genuine sensitivity and concern can easily lead to the dismissal of CSAOs.

Ways to Improve the Evaluation Process

The criteria selected for the evaluation of CSAOs will vary with the objectives of the institution, the priorities of the president, and the specific problems being experienced by students at the time. The following suggestions for enhancing the evaluation of chief student affairs officers should apply in almost all cases, however.

Define the Objectives. Student affairs leaders should ask their presidents to be as explicit as they can in describing their expectations. Ideally, these expectations should be in writing, and should represent what the president and the CSAO have agreed to after considerable discussion. With such an agreement, both administrators can be clear about the goals for student affairs, and may avoid confusion and misunderstanding when campus problems arise. Objectives will vary, by institution, of course, but they should include components in management, problem solving, and education. CSAOs may want to suggest more specific goals they have in mind for the president's consideration.

Agree on Criteria. As McCorkle and Archibald (1982, p. 153) point out, pressures for review of administrative performance have risen sharply, and efforts to develop evaluative criteria are futile without establishing clear objectives. Once the president and the CSAO have agreed on the goals, they must decide how the student affairs leader will be evaluated. A great deal is at stake for CSAOs in the evaluation process, and so it is wise for them to spend considerable time with their presidents in establishing the procedure. Some presidents may prefer to write an annual letter to the CSAO, relying primarily on subjective judgments gained from observation and interaction. Others may become more involved, conducting quarterly discussions with the CSAO and reviewing progress on each of the goals previously set. Some presidents will accept self-evaluations submitted by CSAOs, supported by program assessments carried out during the year. Regardless of the type of institution, presidents will be very sensitive to feedback from faculty, students, community members, the other vice presidents, and others with whom the CSAO has contact. Some may actively seek such feedback as a formal part of the evaluation process, and CSAOs can ask faculty, staff, and student groups to evaluate them and submit their observations to the president.

While it is difficult to describe the performance of CSAOs in statistical terms, some presidents may choose to rate their effectiveness in achieving each of the goals set for them. Thus, CSAOs may be informed that their presidents rate them as excellent in financial management, poor in problem solving, and average in building good educational programs. They might also be rated on their relations with each of the major constituent groups, on their contributions to institutional and community service, on their commitment to affirmative action, and on their sensitivity and concern for students and staff. In any case, as Seldin (1988, p. 216) argues, professional evaluations should not be restricted to one or two administrative functions. Such areas as planning, decision making, ability to deal with people, communication skills, initiative, adaptability, problem solving, and leadership should be included.

Use External Evaluators. Experienced CSAOs are usually not satisfied with the relatively limited evaluations they often receive from their presidents and on-campus colleagues. Even though they may be very helpful, they are done by others who are daily observers of them and who are usually not practicing student affairs professionals. Many CSAOs have convinced their presidents to invite external evaluators to the campus every three or four years to assess their work. This can provide feedback and insights that may not be available in any other way, and has the advantage of bringing new perspectives to the process. External evaluators must of course be given very specific charges, and they must be well informed about the goals and expectations the president has established for the student affairs leader. Such external evaluations may seem threatening to some newly appointed CSAOs who are not well established in their positions. However, this technique is most often suggested by CSAOs themselves, not only to assist their presidents in obtaining independent assessments of their performance but also to improve the quality of their work.

Link Evaluation with Professional Development. CSAOs occupy very risky positions; they have so many diverse constituencies and are confronted with so many problems that their future employment is frequently uncertain. They are not able to control many factors related to their work, and their own professional futures depend largely on the goodwill and support of young undergraduates, whose social and political agendas may change from one year to the next. The hours are long, the stress is high, and there are few immediate tangible rewards. Given this situation, the evaluation process should be linked with the continuing professional development of the CSAO (Munitz, 1980). If the "evaluation" consists of nothing more than a yearly one-page letter from the president notifying the student affairs leader that his or her performance has been acceptable, it serves no useful purpose at all. Or if the evaluation process is feared as a negative experience where all of one's mistakes will be rehashed, it will contribute nothing to improved performance. Unless presidents intend to dismiss their CSAOs, they should use the evaluation process as part of an ongoing program to encourage their professional development. If they are serious about this process, they will need to spend considerable time with their CSAOs, reviewing their performance in detail in relation to previously agreed-on goals. Where shortcomings are noted, specific suggestions or requirements can be made for ways to improve performance. This approach requires that CSAOs become active participants in their own evaluation, and receive assurance that their presidents are genuinely interested in their professional development. Such efforts are likely to build the confidence of CSAOs and stimulate their learning and growth.

Monitor Performance Periodically. It can be very upsetting to CSAOs when the only "evaluation" they receive comes in the middle of a campus crisis, or after a serious problem has been discovered. If this becomes the standard administrative procedure, the student affairs leader will eventually become so cautious and defensive that effective performance will be impossible. Because there are so many difficult and public problems involving students, CSAOs are very vulnerable to this method of evaluation. It leads some of them to feel very insecure in their positions, convinced that their support from their presidents is only as good as the last decision they made. To avoid this very negative situation, presidents should evaluate CSAOs at agreed-on times during the year and in relation to previously established criteria. There may be an hour-long personal evaluation twice per year, and a more lengthy and thorough one completed at the end of the fiscal year. If the president and the CSAO know when the reviews are to occur, both can prepare for them and consider ways to improve performance.

Perhaps worse than only being evaluated in the middle of a campus crisis is being ignored by the president. In the interviews conducted as part of this study, some CSAOs reported that even after two or three years of working for a president, they really did not know how their work was viewed, or whether their continued presence was wanted. A few chief executive officers may want to keep their vice presidents in this insecure state of mind, thinking that they will work harder as a result, but most are so busy that they may not even realize they have not been paying adequate attention to their chief aides. If CSAOs find themselves in this situation, they should be forthright with their presidents, and request periodic and thorough evaluations.

Most presidents will respond favorably, since they want to do everything they can to enhance the performance of their vice presidents.

Use Written Contracts. Another way to build in regular monitoring is to have specific term contracts for the CSAO. A typical contract may be for three years, with particular written expectations and goals as part of the agreement. Toward the end of the contract period, a thorough evaluation would be conducted (perhaps including an external assessment) and a decision would be made whether to continue the CSAO for another contract period. Such arrangements can be beneficial both to CSAOs and to their presidents, because in writing the agreement, they must take part in a good deal of discussion about expectations, goals, and evaluative criteria. A contract can clearly state what each will do to address the needs of the institution's student life program. It can also help CSAOs avoid a serious problem faced by many administrators in high-stress positions — burnout. Contracts have a beginning and an end, and thus may force CSAOs to pay attention to their professional development because they know they may not be in their positions forever. With all of the difficult problems presidents and CSAOs face, contracts may also reduce some of the anxiety CSAOs feel about their jobs and permit them to proceed with their work with confidence. Moreover, they provide the best assurance that presidents will periodically review their performance in accordance with previously agreed-on criteria.

Scrutinize with Rigor. CSAOs deserve every bit as much scrutiny as their colleagues in academic affairs, business affairs, and development. They should expect to be evaluated on the basis of what they accomplish. They cannot claim that there are "no right or wrong answers in student life" as an excuse for their own ineffectiveness as leaders. Just because they may claim to be counselors or behavioral scientists does not excuse them from being held fully accountable for sound fiscal management. It is their responsibility to handle the considerable stress associated with their positions, and not use it as an excuse for indecisiveness or loss of temper. They should accept the fact that their presidents have important agendas to carry out, and that their own priorities may not always match their presidents'. Whatever the issue or problem, they should also understand that it is their obligation to represent their institutions in a positive manner as educational leaders. They must accept the fact that in the volatile world of student affairs, they will inevitably make mistakes and will have to face their critics in the public. They should be expected, too, to exercise good professional judgment even when under heavy scrutiny, and to uphold high ethical standards of behavior in the process. Finally, they should expect to be evaluated in the same rigorous manner they apply to their own staff.

Obstacles to Professional Development

CSAOs are senior administrators at their institutions, and must be mature professionals in order to become appointed to their positions. Most have completed a terminal degree several years before taking the job, and have been so immersed in various positions before becoming CSAOs that they may have spent little time in formal professional development activities. Continuing education is one of the most important professional needs of the CSAOs. The following represent some of the problems associated with this critical function.

Nature of the Position. CSAOs are very susceptible to stress because of long hours, frequent public criticism, and lack of easily definable rewards. Even though they are surrounded by people constantly, the position can be lonely, because there are few others on the campus who share the same level or type of responsibility. The job offers very few opportunities for quiet reflection or planning, and most CSAOs find it difficult to leave the campus for any extended period of time. Most institutions do not grant tenure to student affairs administrators, and so there is often little security associated with the position. All of these factors mitigate against serious professional development, which is too frequently viewed as a supplemental activity, available only when "everything else" has been done. As a result, some CSAOs suffer serious burnout, losing their enthusiasm for the position, experiencing poor health, or feeling as if they have failed.

Institutional Policies. Some colleges and universities may have enlightened professional development opportunities for their faculty but none at all for senior administrators. For example, faculty members may be eligible for formal sabbatical leaves on a periodic basis, but many CSAOs report that they have never had any such option. One student affairs leader joked that if he asked for a six-month leave for professional development, his president would assume he had lost touch with reality! Nevertheless, senior administrators have at least the same need for continuing education and renewal that faculty have, and it is in the best interest of institutions to recognize this need and develop policies that support it. Some institutions are beginning to respond. A number of CSAOs who were interviewed as part of this study reported that their institutions were now encouraging professional development for senior administrators. For example, Michigan State University permits administrators to apply for a three-month professional leave during the summer every four years. Other institutions are also providing financial support for administrators to attend extended professional development workshops specifically designed for them.

Changing Issues. One of the most important needs CSAOs have is to educate themselves about issues facing students, and they cannot fool themselves into thinking that there are easy shortcuts to this. It is a major professional responsibility. However, many of the issues CSAOs must address in the 1990s are very different from those of ten or twenty years ago. How do student affairs leaders remain well informed and sensitive to social, political, legal, and ethical issues? Many of them report that they have little time for professional reading or writing, and that they have to work very hard just to keep up with day-to-day problems. But if they are to be effective leaders, they must not only be aware of what students regard as important issues, they must also have thought seriously about them and must have planned some educational strategies to deal with them. Good programs and services do not result from a hurried, cursory reading of a few short articles on critical issues; they emerge after careful, in-depth study and discussion with others who have done the same.

Need for New Skills. CSAOs in the 1990s have responsibilities for functions that did not exist twenty years ago, that were formerly part of another administrative area, or for which they have received little or no formal preparation. As a result, they have had to learn these skills themselves, or have watched from the sidelines as others who developed the skills assumed more responsibility. For example, CSAOs trained as counselors may now have responsibility for intercollegiate athletics, campus transportation, child care, and campus security. How do they acquire the skills that enable them to administer such programs, and win the necessary confidence of their presidents as they take on these new duties? Other student affairs leaders may have become experts at conflict resolution because of their education and experience in the 1960s and 1970s but are now expected to be astute financial managers. The skills are not the same! Some CSAOs may have spent so many years engaged in administrative problems that they have lost many of their crucial counseling skills. Professional development activities should be directed at upgrading and renewing the skills needed for effective performance.

Absence of Professional Development Requirements. One of the major obstacles student affairs has faced in its efforts to be recognized as a profession is that it places no continuing educational requirements of any kind on its members. Pharmacy, nursing, medicine, law, accounting, and other fields have specific yearly educational requirements for persons to complete if they intend to maintain their professional status. While the advantages and disadvantages of licensure requirements can be debated, the commitment to continuing education by these professions is a sign that professional development is critical to successful performance. It is very difficult for student affairs organizations to enforce any such requirement, though, because there is no standard professional preparation that is common to the field. Moreover, the primary allegiance of CSAOs is to their institutions, not to their professional association. However, the absence of any requirements from the associations has not served CSAOs or the student affairs field well. There is no "yearly reminder" that their own continuing education is critical, and thus such activity is often not given a very high priority. As Cervero (1988) reports, most other professions now embrace the importance of lifelong professional education. It is high time for student affairs to do the same.

"Indispensability." Some CSAOs are so dedicated to their work and so engrossed in their jobs that they convince themselves that they are indispensable. They may think only they can get the job done correctly and thus that they can never leave the campus. These self-appointed martyrs are not only not heroes, but often become obstacles to others' success. Some CSAOs who operate in this fashion may be using this workaholic style to mask professional inadequacies they feel, or to avoid humane, personal interactions with others. Such an approach to the position sets a very poor example for staff, and of course contradicts a serious commitment to professional development. In reality, CSAOs do not remain in their positions forever, and no student affairs leader is indispensable to any institution. But the asumptions of some CSAOs about their indispensability must be recognized as a problem that seriously limits their continuing education.

Desirable Professional Development Activities

Despite the problems just described, there are many ways CSAOs can enhance their professional education and development, and improve their performance in the process. The following examples are presented to illustrate how student affairs leaders can take charge of their own learning.

Teaching. Student affairs leaders should always remember that their most important job is the education of students. This requires them to be actively engaged with ideas, and to be able to communicate these ideas to others effectively. One of the best ways to ensure that this happens is to teach at least one course per year. To do this well requires time and preparation, but it also forces CSAOs to read, think, and organize their ideas in a disciplined way. It also puts them in contact with students in a different setting from the one they are used to in their jobs, and enables them to understand the current classroom realities of their campuses. Most important, teaching can renew CSAOs' commitment to learning as the primary focus of the institution, and can remind them that they should be active contributors to students' education, not just passive observers of it.

Reading, Research, and Writing. Student affairs leaders always seem to be in a hurry, probably because there are so many demands on their time. Like all professionals, they need to schedule some uninterrupted periods during each year to write, read, and test out some fresh ideas concerning their work. If they do not do this, burnout is much more likely to occur, and they may feel they have become slaves to their institutions, unappreciated by others who are insensitive to their personal and professional needs. CSAOs must take responsibility for their own continuing education, and not rely on others to provide it for them. If they are to be contributors to their profession, they must have a strong commitment to this activity. Setting aside time for serious reading, research, and writing is one of the best ways to do this.

Professional Associations. Most CSAOs participate in state, regional, and national associations in student affairs, and many find that these groups provide the most rewarding and valuable professional activities outside their own institutions. The opportunities for leadership and increased awareness of issues are excellent, and the informal contacts made with colleagues often result in the sharing of information and problem-solving techniques. Most student affairs leaders were active in associations for many years before they became CSAOs, and many believe that their involvement in these groups contributed to their professional advancement. As a result, most of them feel an obligation to assist younger staff members who aspire to become chief administrators by encouraging their participation in associations. Assuming leadership in these groups can be time consuming, and CSAOs who choose to do this should make sure it will not adversely affect their campus job performance. They should have the support of their presidents and the understanding of their staff before they agree to accept a major office. In some cases, a visible national office may be pursued for the wrong reason — to seek the positive regard and acclaim that are not earned at the home institution. If this happens, no one benefits. Leadership in associations should be pursued as a potentially valuable volunteer activity, with the objective being a genuine desire to improve the profession. CSAOs who are active in this regard usually find satisfaction with their own continuing education and with the opportunity to participate in the development of their field.

Institutes and Workshops. Many organizations now provide intensive learning experiences for senior administrators in higher education, and CSAOs have been active participants in them. These institutes and workshops have partially grown out of the frustrations with brief professional conferences where participants too often only listened passively to speeches and were not actively engaged with the issues. They also have become popular because of a strongly felt need on the part of CSAOs to address their own educational growth in a serious manner. The Institute for Educational Management at Harvard University offers an intensive four-week summer program for senior college and university administrators. Lectures, case studies, reading, group discussion, and assessments of professional growth make up the activities of the eighty participants. The Institute for Education Management can be especially helpful for CSAOs, because its membership includes other senior administrators, such as presidents, and academic, business, and development officers. The National Association of Student Personnel Administrators also conducts the Richard Stevens Institute each summer, where forty-five CSAOs engage in intensive study and discussion of critical issues in student affairs. A major purpose of the Stevens Institute is professional renewal. With the complex problems being faced by most institutions in the 1990s, professional associations will encounter more demands for workshops on specific issues in student affairs, such as liability and campus security, freedom of expression and harassment, and racial and ethnic awareness. Participation in these institutes and workshops can be a very valuable part of the professional development of CSAOs.

Informal Groups. With the great diversity in colleges and universities, it is not surprising that many small groups of CSAOs have formed over the years, usually representing institutions that share common purposes. These groups rarely have more than twenty-five members, are very informal, and may meet only once or twice per year. However, many CSAOs who are part of such groups say that this is the most valuable professional development activity they have. There are no officers, no speeches, and no opportunities for ego trips. The only reason to form the group is to enhance the learning of the members, through the open sharing of problems and the discussion of issues. These kinds of informal groups are not unique to student affairs, of course, since presidents and other senior administrators have enjoyed similar activities for years. In most such groups, members share information from their campuses with each other in a collegial atmosphere of trust and confidentiality. They also allow administrators to seek advice and counsel from their colleagues, and provide a valuable source of support. So long as these groups remain open to new ideas and do not become exclusive clubs for former leaders, they offer another attractive professional development option to CSAOs.

Professional Leaves. The skills necessary for successful performance as CSAOs are complex and changing. If student affairs leaders are serious about enhancing their management, mediation, and education skills, they and their presidents must recognize that participation in a one-week workshop once every six years just will not get the job done. A semester or even two months during the summer taken as a leave may produce dramatic improvements in certain skills if the professional activity pursued is substantive. It is difficult for CSAOs to justify a leave simply as a respite from the pressures of the position; their objectives should be to learn new skills and gain fresh insights on educational issues. In the process, they often discover new enthusiasm for their work and a readiness to tackle problems that seemed overly daunting only a few months earlier.

CSAOs will rapidly lose their effectiveness as leaders if they do not commit themselves to a planned and rigorous program of professional development. They should seek employment at institutions that expect and support such activity, and should form clear understandings with their presidents about its importance. Their own behavior should serve as a model of commitment to professional growth for their staff. They should also remind themselves to maintain an honest perspective about their own importance and effectiveness, and accept the fact that few CSAOs can best fit the needs of their institutions for all time. Despite their willingness to continue to learn and to grow, they should recognize before their presidents, staff, and students do when it is time to move to another job or institution. The most important task of CSAOs in professional development is to take responsibility for their own continuing education.

Educational Background and Career Paths

What kind of formal preparation is needed to succeed as a CSAO? Is there a preferred career path to the position? The answers to these questions are far more complex in the 1990s than they were thirty years ago, since the number and variety of institutions have multiplied and the diversity of students has increased. The following perspectives on formal preparation and career paths underscore this complexity and diversity.

Formal Preparation. There are excellent discussions of what the content of graduate programs in student affairs administration should be in the literature (Delworth and Hanson, 1989; Brown, 1985; Council for the Advancement of Standards, 1986). However, presidents hire CSAOs, and they are not particularly interested in the internal debates within the profession about the best method of preparation. They know what the needs of their institutions are, and they seek CSAOs whose skills match those needs.

The great majority of CSAOs practicing in the 1990s have a doctorate, but there is very little commonality regarding the content of their graduate work. The primary skills needed for success as student affairs leaders — management, mediation, and education — are learned from a variety of disciplines, so that there is no prescribed path to the CSAO position. Much of the student affairs profession has its roots in counseling and the psychology of individual differences. These fields remain very important to the education of student affairs administrators, but they address only a part of the responsibilities faced by CSAOs. Current graduate programs in student affairs are mainly located in colleges of education. Many of these programs include courses within the college of education that address management, legal, and financial issues, but few students are enrolled in cooperative or joint graduate programs with the colleges of business or law, or schools of management. Because of the diversity of institutions, graduate preparation programs should focus on the special skills CSAOs need at particular types of institutions. CSAOs working at liberal arts colleges should have strong academic backgrounds in a traditional discipline as well as a firm commitment to undergraduate education. Yet few graduate programs in student affairs specifically address this need. Student affairs leaders at community colleges need to be able to work with an extremely diverse student population, and to have excellent mediation and community organization skills. But few of the current graduate programs in student affairs deal directly with the needs of community college CSAOs. The strongest graduate preparation programs in student affairs administration in the next decade will be those that focus on the needs of special kinds of institutions, and those that develop interdisciplinary curricula among multiple academic units.

In practical terms, those who want to become CSAOs should consider their own educational interests and goals and match them with institutions that have the same priorities. Then they should seek graduate programs that prepare them to meet the appropriate job requirements. They should be skeptical of narrowly defined graduate programs that tend to isolate students within single departments and should seek opportunities that enable them to test their ideas and competencies within multiple academic settings. CSAOs must use resources from a great variety of areas and must be able to interact effectively with a large and diverse constituency. The best place to begin learning these skills is in their graduate academic programs.

Career Paths. Aspiring CSAOs should expect to earn a doctorate in a field usually (though not necessarily) related to student affairs, and to have worked for several years in progressively more responsible positions in higher education. Beyond that there is no prescribed career path. A possible career route may be through residence halls, student activities, and student life; it may be through admissions, financial aid, and registration; it may be through teaching in a graduate program in higher education; or it may be through a community or governmental agency. In the interviews conducted as part of this study, CSAOs reported previous positions as directors of admissions, counseling, placement, housing, and college unions; as deans of students, deans of colleges; and professors.

Hiring CSAOs who have followed diverse career paths may frustrate those who value uniformity and who desire to protect the guild from outside barbarians. However, the fact is that many career paths are necessary to meet the very different needs of CSAOs for research universities, liberal arts colleges, urban commuter institutions, and community colleges. Institutions differ with respect to other priorities, too. If a college's most important need is to increase enrollment, it will probably seek a CSAO who has demonstrated success in admissions, recruitment, and financial aid administration. If a university is experiencing racial unrest and political turmoil, it will probably seek a CSAO who has demonstrated strong skills in problem solving and mediation. If presidents are frustrated with sloppy fiscal and organizational problems in student affairs, they will most likely seek CSAOs who have displayed effective management skills in previous positions.

These differing priorities make it clear that aspiring CSAOs need to seek out positions commensurate with their background and goals. Persons seriously interested in a specific CSAO position should become familiar with the history of problems and issues on that campus and should learn why there is an opening, who the president is, and what his or her expectations are. Unless they investigate these matters, candidates have no way of knowing whether their own career paths may logically lead to the open position. But many public advertisements for CSAO positions are written by search committees and are unfortunately so all-encompassing that they provide little useful guidance to candidates about the actual needs and priorities of the institution. Sometimes more intensive research is necessary.

Regardless of the type of institution or its problems, those aspiring to become CSAOs ought to have certain experiences and skills in common. As we have seen, they should be good managers, able to handle organizational, fiscal, and personnel matters with skill; they should be good mediators, able to solve problems and resolve disputes; and they should be effective educators, able to implement successful programs with students and faculty. Competition for CSAO positions is very keen, and the best way to reach that goal is to demonstrate successful performance in other positions. Presidents hire CSAOs because there is clear evidence that they have achieved success as managers, problem solvers, and educators in a responsible position and that they are persons of integrity. There are no automatic stepping-stones to the CSAO job, and those who attempt to use institutions merely to advance their own careers somewhere else are inevitably exposed as self-serving.

As Fisher (1987, p. 417) suggests, just as essential as finding the right leaders for higher education is helping to develop, motivate, and nourish them. There are many exciting and rewarding continuing education opportunities for CSAOs, as well as increasing recognition that the skills necessary to achieve success in the position can be learned from a variety of academic disciplines and through a number of different career paths. The most successful CSAOs are those who have developed clear agreements with their presidents about how their performance will be evaluated and what the specific expectations are for their positions. They are also the ones who take responsibility for their own professional education and growth, ensuring that they do not become so captured by the job that they cannot continue to learn.

9

Student Affairs Leaders
for Tomorrow

The CSAO position has acquired a major administrative role in higher education in the past thirty years. It represents the efforts of institutions to coordinate various student services and functions and to improve the overall quality of student life. The responsibilities of the position have become very extensive and now include departments not previously part of traditional student affairs organizations. With these increased responsibilities have come considerable visibility and high expectations for performance. CSAOs have retained their traditional roles as advocates of student needs and as service providers; however, they are now expected to be good managers, mediators, and educators as well. They no longer function on the sidelines of the institution but are active participants in the educational and public life of their colleges. They do not occupy a safe and noncontroversial corner of the campus where they pursue their own agendas; they are visible leaders who have to be responsive to many constituencies in addition to their students. The position is now enjoying the highest level of influence in its brief history. As demands for services increase and problems continue to surface, additional responsibilities will emerge that will require the attention of current practitioners, graduate program faculty, and institutional presidents. The purposes of this chapter are to review the hallmarks of the competent CSAO, to survey trends and issues that will affect the position in the future, and to consider the implications of these insights for the presidents who supervise CSAOs, the educators who prepare professionals for the student affairs field, and the men and women who aspire to become CSAOs themselves.

Hallmarks of the Competent CSAO

As stated earlier, CSAOs exist for the education of students. Their academic preparation, administrative style, and organizational strategy should all be directed toward this most important goal. The particular emphasis they give to their position will vary with the academic and social goals and traditions of their institutions. Regardless of the college or university, however, all of them must demonstrate competence in three major roles: manager, mediator, and educator. If they fail at any one of these critical functions, they cannot achieve success. The educational preparation they receive before becoming CSAOs is extremely important and should assist them in gaining expertise in the three major areas of responsibility the position requires. These skills can be learned from a variety of academic disciplines, and CSAOs will thus be appointed from a wide range of educational and administrative backgrounds. It is also important for CSAOs to be well informed about student cultures, the history and philosophy of higher education, and the particular heritage and purposes of their own institutions.

The most important of the three major functions of CSAOs is education. To be effective in this role, student affairs leaders must give thoughtful consideration to the developmental needs of students in relation to the academic and social goals of the institution. The most effective CSAOs are actively engaged with the academic programs of their college and are also involved in systematic efforts to assess students' educational progress.

Moreover, successful CSAOs are sensitive and responsive to the various constituencies associated with their positions: students, faculty, the community, parents, the governing board, the legislature and the federal government, donors and alumni, and the student affairs staff. Not only are they visible to these groups, but they assume an active role in helping them learn about the needs of students and the institution. The best CSAOs are able to earn the support and understanding of these constituencies and recognize that their own success is very dependent on the way they are perceived by them.

Colleges and universities vary widely in the composition and academic preparation of their students, the breadth of their curricula, their geographical location, their educational and social goals, and their available financial resources. Successful CSAOs know that their primary commitment must be to their institutions and that their backgrounds and skills should match the needs of the institution. Research universities, urban commuter institutions, liberal arts colleges, and community colleges are very different from one another, and few CSAOs have skills that fit them all. The best student affairs leaders understand that their skills and interests are best suited to a particular type of college or university.

The most competent and successful CSAOs are also teachers for their students and staff. The actions they take, the way they make decisions, the concern they show for others, and the way they continue to learn as professionals often can serve as a model for others. Because of their visibility on their campuses, the compassion they demonstrate for students may have a strong impact on others. Above all, the best CSAOs show a daily commitment to integrity in everything they do, and understand that their effectiveness depends on the trust they are able to earn from others.

On a more personal level, the most successful CSAOs pay close attention to their own physical and mental health needs, since they recognize that the long hours and frequent public criticism they absorb can take their toll. They have realistic notions of their own abilities and limitations and stay in the position only as long as they enjoy it and feel they can serve their institutions effectively. They maintain a positive and enthusiastic commitment to their work, always seeking solutions to problems, as opposed to complaining about all the difficulties. They have genuine affection for students, and are able to see potential for good in all of them.

To be successful and to accomplish the many different goals of the position, CSAOs must be leaders. Everything else depends on this quality. There are many different styles of leadership, and CSAOs do not become leaders simply by holding the position. They must initiate ideas and proposals and see that they are implemented successfully.

Perhaps most important, the best CSAOs understand students, are sensitive to their special needs, and win their trust and confidence. Student affairs administration is a very personal endeavor, and programs, policies, and organizational charts can never take the place of concern for individual students. Regardless of the size or type of institution, CSAOs must remember that their first priority is the education of students, and to be successful at this, they must become close to them.

Such qualities and characteristics will increasingly be put to the test in coming years. Major changes will require creative solutions in the field of student affairs.

Emerging Trends

The agenda of higher education always reflects the aspirations, priorities, and current problems of society. This is perhaps even more the case for student affairs than it is for the formal curriculum. In the past thirty years, the major influences on student affairs have been external to the campus: the civil rights movement, the rising expectations for higher education, the Vietnam War, and the national political trend (since 1980) toward conservatism. All of these factors have altered the roles of CSAOs. Because of society's changing priorities, hundreds of new community colleges were established during these years to address the needs of students not previously served by traditional colleges and universities. CSAOs in these new institutions often assumed responsibility for academic support and community liaison programs, duties not traditionally part of student affairs. They also learned to assist older, part-time students, who were very different from the eighteen- to twenty-four-year-old population that had been dominant for so long.

All of this shows that student affairs administrators must be responsive to major trends and issues in order to serve their students effectively. It is impossible to predict international events or economic conditions, but such events as the war in the Persian Gulf or a national recession certainly have an impact on campus life and hence on the CSAO.

Changing Demographics. Students will reflect the changes in the overall population, and there will be much more diversity in college and university enrollments. In some states, the term *minority* will take on new meaning, since those now defined as minority students will outnumber others. In other states, decreases in the traditional-age population will continue, and institutions will most likely seek nontraditional (usually older) students to survive. The trend toward part-time students will probably continue, and, mostly owing to economic factors, students will attend colleges relatively close to where they live. Foreign students will increase in number, with the largest component coming from the Pacific Rim countries. All these factors will be very important to CSAOs, who will have to monitor changes in the student population for their campuses. They will often serve as "interpreters" to the faculty, staff, and governing boards of their institutions regarding the shifting student demographics, explaining what is happening and urging necessary adjustments in programs, policies, and facilities. They will have to develop greater sensitivity to and awareness of the various student cultures on their campuses, and prove that they can earn the confidence and support of each of them. They must also be prepared to deal with the inevitable conflicts that will arise as diverse groups compete for access and resources. CSAOs will need to be more involved in their communities, reaching out to the various groups that can provide understanding and support in meeting the needs of students. They will also be expected to provide strong leadership in efforts to recruit, retain, and graduate students. These changing demographics will mean that CSAOs will be hired from more diverse backgrounds, and that their educational preparation will need to include a strong emphasis on student diversity. At the same time, the need for continuing professional development will be extremely strong, because CSAOs will have to work hard to stay current with changing student populations.

Racial and Ethnic Relations. Racism has been one of the most persistent and difficult problems in American society for generations. Because of the growing diversity of students, the tensions in racial and ethnic relations in society as a whole are increasingly being reflected on college campuses, and there are few indications that those tensions will disappear soon. Clashes over admissions standards, housing policies, financial aid, hiring policies, and student activities are likely to intensify, and all these problems affect student affairs leaders, who are expected to prevent or solve them. CSAOs should not view racial and ethnic tensions as insurmountable obstacles. They must be prepared to provide leadership in this area; they will need to have a positive vision of a racially harmonious campus and the courage and determination to work toward that goal. Student affairs leaders hired in the next decade should have academic and experiential backgrounds that prepare them for multicultural education, since presidents will look for CSAOs who can work effectively with a racially diverse student body. They will also seek out student affairs leaders with well-developed mediation skills and the ability to enlist the participation of many diverse groups in problem-solving efforts.

Gender-Related Issues. On most campuses, awareness of sexual assault, acquaintance rape, and sexual abuse is growing. Programs emphasizing education, prevention, and treatment are increasing in number, and CSAOs will need to assume strong leadership to assure that such programs are supported and well understood. It will be the responsibility of student affairs leaders to initiate such programs, to see that they are funded adequately, and to supervise them effectively. The most successful efforts will involve both men and women students and will include participation by legal, medical, psychological, law enforcement, and student affairs personnel. Various forms of sexual violence and exploitation are present on many campuses, and CSAOs will increasingly be expected to develop policies and programs to prevent them. CSAOs need to be sensitive to the ways in which men and women students interact on their campuses and to be willing to deal with difficult problems in spite of pressures from those who would prefer to ignore or disguise them.

Costs. CSAOs always have to worry about money, because it is necessary for them to hire staff, develop programs, and build and maintain facilities. The availability of funds can also have a major impact on the composition of the student body, as tuition levels are set and as scholarship and recruiting dollars are allocated. It is very likely that student, parent, and governmental concern over college costs will continue to escalate in the next decade. As a result, CSAOs will need to become more aggressive and creative in their efforts to identify and use financial resources. They will certainly have to consider increased student user fees, external fund raising, and contracted services as alternative ways to make services available to students, because institutional budgets may not be able to support all the demands. Student affairs leaders will need to become more visible and influential with legislatures and governing boards that make policies directly affecting funding. To ensure a diverse and economically balanced student body, CSAOs will have to be very persuasive with their presidents to secure the funds needed to recruit and enroll students. Good financial management is a necessity for CSAOs, but in addition, they will be expected to identify and obtain a significant portion of the funds needed to carry out their programs. This need will influence the kinds of persons hired for the position, and will affect those responsible for graduate preparation programs as well. Student affairs leaders will actively seek professional development opportunities that help them learn the needed skills.

Health Issues. There is widespread concern now about health issues: stress, drug and alcohol abuse, anorexia and bulimia, and AIDS, and this concern is likely to intensify in the next decade. Thus student affairs leaders will have to be very well informed about health issues and able to convince their presidents that enlightened policies regarding these issues are necessary. And they will need continuing education about health matters, not just to be able to respond to all the demands and problems that arise, but also to develop comprehensive campus programs designed to encourage and support good health. CSAOs will be expected to make additional services available to students, and to establish policies that provide for the participation and rehabilitation of students with health-related problems. Such new programs will require additional staff, money, and physical facilities; and the responsibility for locating the resources will be the CSAO's. Since few institutions have enough money to meet the seemingly unending demands for physical and mental health services, CSAOs will often make contractual agreements with local hospitals and other health care agencies to provide the services.

Computers and Other New Technology. Because student affairs is such a people-oriented profession, many CSAOs have not taken the time to understand the many ways computers and other forms of technology can be used to improve their services and programs. They have often simply delegated authority for such activities to someone on their staff and have paid little attention to the area, even though their success as administrators may depend on doing so. In the next decade, the revolution in computer technology will certainly continue, and new methods of processing information, communicating with students, and delivering services will be made available to institutions. Students themselves will be increasingly sophisticated in such matters, and will expect their colleges and universities to meet their needs. All of this will require CSAOs who are competent in the use of computers and other technological tools. The stakes are too high for them to become completely dependent on the expertise of specialists in this area. They must understand what is needed, the various options available, and the best and most economical ways to deliver it. The call for technological competence has strong implications for the education of future CSAOs and their continuing professional development. It is also very likely that presidents will want to hire student affairs leaders who have demonstrated that they have these skills.

Student Behavior. The popular press may claim that in loco parentis disappeared in the 1960s and 1970s, but most CSAOs would strongly dispute any such notion. They remain responsible for extensive student judicial programs, and most colleges and universities are still expected to intervene when there are student disturbances, to curb alcohol and drug abuse, and to prevent assaults and vandalism. Whenever such problems occur, the CSAO is expected to see that strong and timely actions are taken to correct them. There is now widespread concern about campus security, rape, theft, and substance abuse, and there are few signs that such problems will decrease in the next decade. At the same time, there is a resurgence of interest in teaching positive values to students. This is reflected in a widespread public conviction that colleges should somehow eliminate the negative attitudes students may have, such as racism and sexism. CSAOs are in the midst of this fray, and the action surely will intensify in the next few years. Courage, patience, and competence in problem solving will be required, along with the ability to withstand harsh criticism. Presidents are certain to take such factors into account in their decisions to hire CSAOs, and professional preparation programs will need to include major components on student behavior and values development in their curricula. Professional development programs will continue to proliferate, as CSAOs understand the strong need to improve their skills in handling such problems.

Undergraduate Education Reform. A large number of colleges and universities are now examining their undergraduate programs, particularly the general education requirements. This scrutiny is largely a response to the national reports issued in the past six years, each of which has called for major changes in what students study and learn. During the next decade, it is very likely that significant reforms will be introduced on scores of campuses, and CSAOs should be active participants in these efforts. They cannot claim to contribute in very important ways to the education of their students if they are not involved in the discussions and plans to implement changes in the general studies program. This means, of course, that CSAOs must have something of substance to contribute. Their knowledge of student cultures, their experience in developing student leadership, their awareness of special student needs, and their focus on student outcomes all can be of considerable value to committees charged with improving undergraduate education. CSAOs must be well informed about these issues, and should be able to make cogent and persuasive proposals to faculty about what they think students should learn. Student affairs leaders will consequently have to be very familiar with the academic programs at their institutions, with the faculty members who are involved in efforts to improve the undergraduate program, and with similar activities on other campuses. Presidents take it for granted that CSAOs will be experts in student affairs when they hire them; in the coming decade, they will also expect them to be active in improving undergraduate education. This reality has clear implications for professional preparation programs, which currently focus mainly on problems and issues that arise within the student affairs division. During conversations with many CSAOs, it became apparent that they recognized the need for professional development concerning the curriculum but felt that they had to look outside the student affairs associations to find it. The emerging interest in improving the teaching and learning process for undergraduates will present great opportunities for CSAOs to extend their influence as leaders in the next decade. If they prepare themselves well, they can be participants in this very exciting and promising effort.

Student affairs administrators have always had to adjust and respond to the changing needs of students and their institutions. The best CSAOs in the next decade will carefully watch trends and issues in the larger society, and will try to anticipate their impact upon the campus. They will work hard to gain new insights and learn new skills needed to address emerging issues and problems. They will understand that presidents will hire CSAOs who can provide strong leadership in the management, mediation, and education functions of the position, and will expect them to anticipate major campus issues before they become insurmountable problems. They will recognize and accept the dynamic nature of their positions, and the increasing expectations presidents, faculty, students, and others have for them. Their titles may remain the same, but they will be expected to contribute to the improvement of their institutions in areas outside the traditional student affairs program. The next decade may be the most exciting and challenging time in the brief history of the CSAO position, because of the rising expectations for services, the difficulty of the problems higher education faces, and the proven record of sound performance by so many current CSAOs. Successful performance will require creative and dedicated leaders who know the issues, have excellent skills, and have a strong commitment to the education of students.

Other Major Challenges Ahead. As indicated by the Carnegie Association study on the campus community (Boyer, 1990), there is widespread concern about the quality of life for students throughout the nation. Few CSAOs were surprised at any of the findings of this study, because they are so close to the actual daily problems and experiences of students. However, they are pleased that such problems as racism, sexism, substance abuse, stress, and fragmented undergraduate studies are receiving the kind of national exposure the Carnegie study has given them, since it can certainly stimulate wider discussion of these problems, and should lead to improvements in campus social and academic life. All of the problems facing the future of higher education bear directly on the role of the CSAO and pose major challenges in this decade. The best student affairs leaders will prepare themselves for these challenges through intensive professional development and further education. They will need to have the intellectual and leadership skills to improve the quality of student life, even as they face the very difficult problems ahead. With all the pressures and challenges of the position, they must maintain their loyalty to their institutions and to their presidents. Yet they should also understand that with the changing needs, there will come a time when their own skills and professional priorities will not fit well with those of their institutions. When that happens, it will be time to move elsewhere.

Ensuring Competent CSAOs for Tomorrow

At the risk of seeming presumptuous, I offer the following thoughts in the form of advice to current colleagues, presidents, and those who may seek the CSAO position in the next decade.

The President's Role

Very few CSAOs can achieve success without the support and understanding of their presidents. When presidents appoint new student affairs leaders, they should look for administrators who have already demonstrated their skills at management, mediation, and education. Presidents should not be restricted in their hiring decisions by unwieldy and often uninformed search committees that have little understanding of the position. They should accept helpful advice from such groups but should assert their own priorities to secure the right person for the job, seeking candidates from a variety of academic disciplines and experiential backgrounds, even if the decision will perhaps be unpopular with those who would restrict access to CSAO positions to those with a narrowly specific education. The focus should be on the necessary leadership skills, and not on any exclusive academic field that claims it has a monopoly on producing such skills. Presidents should make it as clear as possible what it is they expect from their CSAOs, and they need to provide them with regular feedback on their progress in meeting agreed-on goals. The worst fear of CSAOs is that they will be ignored by their presidents; they need and can handle vigorous, critical evaluation of their work. Their excellent performance should be rewarded, and their shortcomings should be confronted directly. Presidents should also recognize the strong needs of CSAOs for educational and professional renewal and should push their student affairs leaders to take advantage of the many opportunities available. In hiring a CSAO, presidents should seek the best fit between the person and the institution, recognizing that certain student affairs leaders can work well in one setting but not in another. The overwhelming majority of presidents do not have the time or inclination to deal with student problems and issues on a daily basis. They deserve to have CSAOs who will take charge of their division and give strong leadership to it. Presidents should seek CSAOs who are able and willing to make difficult and sometimes unpopular decisions, and to bear responsibility for them — to take the heat. At the same time, presidents need to establish a trusting relationship with their CSAOs, since their support, especially in times of turmoil, is critical to student affairs leaders' success. Presidents do not have to become close friends with their CSAOs, but they should know them well enough to recognize when they need a little humor, some compassion, or a critical review. For CSAOs, knowing that their presidents are paying attention and understand what they are doing is extremely important. Presidents should expect their CSAOs to work hard and to be loyal to them and to the institution. They can achieve the best results by making it clear what they expect, and by evaluating the work of the CSAOs carefully and on a regular basis.

The Roles and Objectives of Professional Education Programs

CSAOs now hold regular and useful conversations with faculty who are responsible for graduate programs in higher education and student affairs. It is acknowledged that none of these graduate programs has as its primary objective the preparation of chief student affairs officers. Most of them properly focus their efforts on substantive educational issues and concepts, not simply on job training. Moreover, most of the students enrolled in graduate programs will assume entry-level or middle-management level positions on completion of their degrees and will not compete for chief student affairs officer positions for several years. However, faculty of graduate and professional programs will benefit by listening closely to CSAOs, observing their actual leadership behavior, and understanding the challenges they are facing.

Graduate programs in higher education and student affairs can also serve future student affairs leaders well by helping them become confident leaders in the management, mediation, and educational roles they will assume. Many of the CSAOs with whom I spoke felt that the focus of their graduate study had been too narrow and had not addressed some of the most critically needed skills, especially in the management and mediation areas. This situation offers a fine opportunity for student affairs leaders and graduate program faculty members to develop cooperative programs from which both can benefit.

Closing Advice to the Aspiring CSAO

The position of CSAO is still evolving, and because of the changing nature of the problems and issues that officer confronts, the job will certainly be different in the next decade from what it is now. Advice offered by a current practitioner, even augmented by helpful comments from many colleagues, necessarily reflects present perceptions and experiences. Nevertheless, the following thoughts may prove useful. The advice is personal and is thus addressed to "you."

Know Yourself. You should assess your own priorities and preferred life-style, and honestly and realistically decide if they will accord well with being a CSAO. If your goal is power, prestige, or money, you have selected the wrong field. However, if you have a genuine desire to exercise leadership in education, then you are on the right track. Many CSAOs have come from faculty, counseling, or middle-management backgrounds, have found the position very unsatisfying, and have left it after a short time. This has usually been because they did not think carefully about what the position really entailed or take a close look at their own abilities and personal priorities. They often found that the long hours, the frequent criticism, and the necessity to make unpopular decisions made them very uncomfortable. There is nothing wrong with these feelings; the job is not for everyone — so be honest with yourself about what you are really like, and if that meshes with the requirements of the CSAO's position, pursue it!

Have a Philosophy. If you have not taken the time over the years to formulate a clear, coherent point of view about what you think the main tasks of higher education are, the CSAO position is not for you. To accomplish anything of value as a student affairs leader, you have to be able to persuade others — students, faculty, staff, parents, community members, and your president — of the worthiness of your educational and social goals. This requires not only a genuine and passionate commitment to education but also years of serious reading and thinking about specific ideas and problems in higher education. The first question you will probably be asked by a president thinking of hiring you is "What would you like to accomplish in this job?" The ability to articulate a coherent and credible rationale will probably determine whether you get the job, and how successful you will be once you are in it. Trendy phrases or catchy psychological jargon will not only not persuade anyone; it will also expose you as a person of little substance. If you want to be a CSAO, you will need to develop a philosophy of education, believe in it sincerely, be able to defend it, and learn how to convince others of its importance.

Pay Your Dues. While there are many career paths to the CSAO position, there is no easy route. Skills in management, mediation, and education are learned, and presidents will only consider candidates for the job who have already demonstrated proficiency in these areas in previous positions. There simply is no substitute for this experience. Paying your dues also means having the terminal degree in an appropriate field and presenting clear evidence of commitment to your own continuing professional education. Talking about the skills and education you have is easy and usually unconvincing; successful performance in jobs related to the CSAO position at the specific institution is the key.

Select Your Institution. Poor fit between the CSAO and the institution is probably the major reason for failure in the position. Your educational philosophy must match the purposes and goals of the college. CSAOs in Ivy League universities, large state universities, urban commuter institutions, and rural community colleges should have very different backgrounds, goals, and styles. Too many CSAOs have been influenced to accept their positions by the prestige, location, or pay scale of the institution. When their own educational priorities, intellectual skills, or social sophistication do not match their institution's, no one is happy, and failure is the usual result. Very few CSAOs achieve success at colleges that differ significantly from their previous institution. Think carefully about the type of college or university where your priorities and skills will fit, and where you can feel confident that your efforts will be appreciated.

Be Willing to Move. In the interviews conducted as part of this study, only four CSAOs out of thirty-five reported that they had previously worked at the institution where they became the student affairs leader. Most had worked at at least two other colleges, and all reported that such experience was critical to their own learning and marketability. Many commented that working at other institutions had helped them shed some of their educational provincialism and made them more confident in their ability to adapt to new people and new settings. It is possible, but unlikely, that you might work your way up over the years at your own institution and become the CSAO. To broaden your perspective, build your professional confidence, and increase your chances, you should be willing to move to progressively more responsible positions at similar types of institutions.

Select Your President. The fit with the institution is very important, but there will be trouble if you and the president do not get along well. You may think you are so adaptable and likable that you can make any relationship work; however, if your administrative style and approach to students are at odds with your president's, you will experience great frustration and probable failure. Before you consider visiting a campus for an interview, inquire about the president and learn about his or her educational background and previous positions. Before you accept any CSAO position, spend a good deal of time with the president, and be very candid about yourself and your intended approach to the job. Discuss with the president how he or she will work with you and what will be expected of you. It is much better to make this frank assessment before accepting the position than it is to discover three months into the job that you are incompatible with the president. It may feel awkward at the time, but you owe it to yourself to do this.

Maintain Your Health. Senior administrative positions in higher education are taxing to your physical and emotional health. It is easy to be overwhelmed by the stress associated with the job of CSAO. Strain is almost always reflected in poor relations with staff, impatience and anger with students, and sloppy decision making on campus. The stress of the position will not go away; the best way to deal with it is to maintain good physical and emotional health, whether through regular physical exercise, outside hobbies, or just time alone. No one else can do this for you; despite your busy schedule, you have to do it for yourself.

Love the Students. If you are uncomfortable with students, irritated by their behavior, or bored by their intellectual immaturity, then you should pursue another career. Students are extremely perceptive and know if the CSAO really cares about them and enjoys being with them. There are hundreds of student events that CSAOs should attend each year, and each provides an opportunity to demonstrate genuine interest and enthusiasm for what the students are doing. The best CSAOs have a real affection for students and pursue their jobs with vigor and good humor, not out of a sense of stoic drudgery. If you aspire to be a CSAO, start with a fundamental love for students and their education.

Overriding Priorities of the Office

Regardless of the type, location, or purpose of their institutions, CSAOs exist for the education of students. They should be the most articulate, informed, and persuasive advocates for students' education on their campuses. Their success is a function of their leadership capacity, and of their ability to understand and gain the confidence and support of a number of constituent groups. They must be good managers, mediators, and educators, and they must know how to work effectively as a part of the institution's management team. They must have compassion for students and must understand that everything they do depends on their integrity and the personal trust they establish with others. Their major responsibility is to do everything they can to make their colleges work for the education of their students.

REFERENCES

American Association of State Colleges and Universities. *To Secure the Blessings of Liberty: A Report on the Role and Future of State Colleges and Universities.* Washington, D.C.: American Association of State Colleges and Universities, 1986.

American Council on Education. *The Student Personnel Point of View.* Washington, D.C.: American Council on Education, 1937.

Argyris, C. *Reasoning, Learning, and Action: Individual and Organizational.* San Francisco: Jossey-Bass, 1982.

Association of American Colleges. *Integrity in the College Curriculum: A Report to the College Community.* Washington, D.C.: Association of American Colleges, 1985.

Astin, A. W. *Four Critical Years: Effects of College on Beliefs, Attitudes, and Knowledge.* San Francisco: Jossey-Bass, 1977.

Baldridge, J. V., and Deal, T. *The Dynamics of Organizational Change in Education.* Berkeley, Calif.: McCutchan, 1983.

Banning, J. "Creating a Climate for Successful Student Development: The Campus Ecology Manager." In U. Delworth, G. R. Hanson, and Associates, *Student Services: A Handbook for the Profession.* (2nd ed.) San Francisco: Jossey-Bass, 1989.

Barzun, J. "Deans Within Deans." *Atlantic Monthly,* Feb. 1945, pp. 75–81.

Bennett, W. J. *Study Group on the State of Learning in the Humanities in Higher Education: To Reclaim a Legacy.* Washington, D.C.: National Endowment for the Humanities, 1985.

Blake, R. R., and Mouton, J. S. *Solving Costly Organizational Conflicts: Achieving Intergroup Trust, Cooperation, and Teamwork.* San Francisco: Jossey-Bass, 1984.

Bloom, A. *The Closing of the American Mind*. New York: Simon & Schuster, 1987.

Bolman, L. G., and Deal, T. E. *Modern Approaches to Understanding and Managing Organizations*. San Francisco: Jossey-Bass, 1984.

Boyer, E. L. *College: The Undergraduate Experience in America*. New York: Harper & Row, 1987.

Boyer, E. L. *Campus Life: In Search of Community*. Lawrenceville, N.J.: Princeton University Press, 1990.

Briggs, L. R. "Some Old Fashioned Doubts About New Fashioned Education." *Atlantic Monthly*, Oct. 1900, pp. 463–470.

Brooks, G. D., and Avila, J. F. "The Chief Student Personnel Administrator and His Staff: A Profile." *NASPA Journal*, 1974, *11*, 41–47.

Brown, R. D. *Student Development in Tomorrow's Higher Education: A Return to the Academy*. Washington, D.C.: American College Personnel Association, 1972.

Brown, R. D. "Graduate Education for the Student Development Educator: A Content and Process Model." *NASPA Journal*, 1985, *22*, 38–43.

Brown, R. W. *Dean Briggs*. New York: Harper & Row, 1926.

Brown, S. S. "Approaches to Collaboration Between Academic and Student Affairs: An Overview." *NASPA Journal*, 1989, *26*, 2–7.

Canon, H. J. "Developing Staff Potential." In U. Delworth, G. R. Hanson, and Associates, *Student Services: A Handbook for the Profession*. San Francisco: Jossey-Bass, 1980.

Cervero, R. M. *Effective Continuing Education for Professionals*. San Francisco: Jossey-Bass, 1988.

Chickering, A. W. *Education and Identity*. San Francisco: Jossey-Bass, 1969.

Chickering, A. W. *Commuting Versus Resident Students: Overcoming Education Inequities of Living Off Campus*. San Francisco: Jossey-Bass, 1974.

Council for the Advancement of Standards. "Environmental and Specialty Standards for Student Affairs Practice in Higher Education." In *Standards for Student Services/Development Programs*. Athens: Council for the Advancement of Standards, University of Georgia, 1986.

Cowley, W. H. "The Disappearing Dean of Men." In *Secretarial Notes, 19th annual conference of the National Association of Deans and Advisers of Men.* Austin: University of Texas, 1937.

Cowley, W. H. "Some History and a Venture in Prophecy." In E. G. Williamson (ed.), *Trends in Student Personnel Work.* Minneapolis: University of Minnesota Press, 1949.

Crookston, B. B. "The Nomenclature Dilemma: Titles of Principal Student Affairs Officers at NASPA Institutions." *NASPA Journal,* 1974, *11,* 3–6.

Dahl, R. *Who Governs?* New Haven, Conn.: Yale University Press, 1961.

Daniels, T. D., and Spiker, B. K. *Perspectives on Organizational Communication.* Dubuque, Iowa: Brown, 1987.

Delworth, U., and Hanson, G. R. "Structure of the Profession and Recommended Curriculum." In U. Delworth, G. R. Hanson, and Associates, *Student Services: A Handbook for the Profession.* (2nd ed.) San Francisco: Jossey-Bass, 1989.

Delworth, U., Hanson, G. R., and Associates. *Student Services: A Handbook for the Profession.* (1st ed.) San Francisco: Jossey-Bass, 1980.

Deutsch, M. *The Resolution of Conflict.* New Haven, Conn.: Yale University Press, 1973.

Education Commission of the States. *Transforming the State Role in Undergraduate Education: Time for a Different View.* Denver, Colo.: Education Commission of the States, 1986.

Ehrle, E. B., and Bennett, J. B. *Managing the Academic Enterprise.* New York: A.C.E./Macmillan, 1988.

Feldman, K. A., and Newcomb, T. M. *The Impact of College on Students.* San Francisco: Jossey-Bass, 1969.

Fenske, R. H. "Historical Foundations of Student Services." In U. Delworth, G. R. Hanson, and Associates, *Student Services: A Handbook for the Profession.* (2nd ed.) San Francisco: Jossey-Bass, 1989.

Fisher, C. F. "Leadership Selection, Evaluation, and Development." In M. W. Peterson and L. A. Mets (eds.), *Key Resources on Higher Education Governance, Management, and Leadership: A Guide to the Literature.* San Francisco: Jossey-Bass, 1987.

Fisher, J. L. *Power of the Presidency.* New York: Macmillan, 1984.

Fisher, R., and Ury, W. *Getting to Yes.* New York: Penguin Books, 1983.

Fley, J. "LeBaron Russell Briggs: He Meant Harvard." *Journal of the National Association of Women Deans, Administrators, and Counselors,* 1977, *41,* 21–24.

Fley, J. "Marion Talbot and the Great Adventure at Chicago." *Journal of the National Association of Women Deans, Administrators, and Counselors,* 1978, *41,* 81–83.

Folberg, J., and Taylor, A. *Mediation: A Comprehensive Guide to Resolving Conflicts Without Litigation.* San Francisco: Jossey-Bass, 1984.

Gerstein, A., and Reagan, J. *Win–Win: Approaches to Conflict Resolution.* Salt Lake City, Utah: Peregrine Smith Books, 1986.

Gilley, J. W., Fulmer, K. A., and Reithlingsbroefer, S. J. *Searching for Academic Excellence: Twenty Colleges and Universities on the Move and Their Leaders.* New York: A.C.E./Macmillan, 1986.

Gilmore, T. H. *Making a Leadership Change: How Organizations and Leaders Can Handle Leadership Transitions Successfully.* San Francisco: Jossey-Bass, 1988.

Gray, B. *Collaborating: Finding Ground for Multiparty Problems.* San Francisco: Jossey-Bass, 1989.

Himes, J. S. *Conflict and Conflict Management.* Athens: University of Georgia Press, 1980.

Holmes, L. *A History of the Position of Dean of Women in a Selected Group of Coeducational Colleges and Universities in the United States.* New York: Teachers College, 1939.

Houle, C. O. *Continuing Learning in the Professions.* San Francisco: Jossey-Bass, 1980.

Hyatt, J. H., and Santiago, A. A. *Financial Management of Colleges and Universities.* Washington, D.C.: National Association of College and University Business Officers, 1986.

Kauffman, J. F. *At the Pleasure of the Board: The Service of the College and University President.* Washington, D.C.: American Council on Education, 1980.

Keller, G. *Academic Strategy: The Management Revolution in American Higher Education.* Baltimore, Md.: Johns Hopkins University Press, 1983.

Kerr, C. *The Uses of the University.* (3rd ed.) Cambridge, Mass.: Harvard University Press, 1982.

Kerr, C. *Presidents Make a Difference: Strengthening Leadership in Colleges and Universities.* Washington, D.C.: Association of Governing Boards, 1984.

Kerr, C., and Gade, M. L. *The Many Lives of Academic Presidents: Time, Place, and Character.* Washington, D.C.: Association of Governing Boards, 1986.

Kerr, R. A. "Evaluating the Services." In U. Delworth, G. R. Hanson, and Associates, *Student Services: A Handbook for the Profession.* San Francisco: Jossey-Bass, 1980.

Knefelkamp, L., Widick, C., and Parker, C. A. (eds.). *Applying New Developmental Findings.* New Directions for Student Services, no. 4. San Francisco: Jossey-Bass, 1978.

Knock, G. H. "Development of Student Services in Higher Education." In M. J. Barr, L. A. Keating, and Associates, *Developing Effective Student Services Programs: Systematic Approaches for Practitioners.* San Francisco: Jossey-Bass, 1985.

Kohlberg, L. *The Philosophy of Moral Development.* San Francisco: Harper & Row, 1981.

Kouzes, J. M., and Posner, B. Z. *The Leadership Challenge: How to Get Extraordinary Things Done in Organizations.* San Francisco: Jossey-Bass, 1987.

Kuh, G. D., Evans, N. J., and Duke, A. "Career Paths and Responsibilities of Chief Student Affairs Officers." *NASPA Journal,* 1983, *21,* 39–47.

Leonard, E. A. *Origins of Personnel Services in American Higher Education.* Minneapolis: University of Minnesota Press, 1956.

Lloyd-Jones, E. "The Beginnings of Our Profession." In E. G. Williamson (ed.), *Trends in Student Personnel Work.* Minneapolis: University of Minnesota Press, 1949.

Lunsford, L. W. "The Chief Student Affairs Officer: Ladder to the Top." *NASPA Journal,* 1984, *22,* 48–56.

McCorkle, C. O., Jr., and Archibald, S. O. *Management and Leadership in Higher Education: Applying Modern Techniques of Planning, Resource Management, and Evaluation.* San Francisco: Jossey-Bass, 1982.

Mathews, L. K. *The Dean of Women.* Boston: Houghton Mifflin, 1915.

Miller, T. K., and Prince, J. S. *The Future of Student Affairs: A*

Guide to Student Development for Tomorrow's Higher Education. San Francisco: Jossey-Bass, 1976.

Millett, J. D. *The Academic Community.* New York: McGraw-Hill, 1962.

Mitchell, A. A., and Roof, M. "Student Affairs and Faculty Partnerships: Dismantling Barriers." *NASPA Journal,* 1988, *26,* 278–283.

Moden, G. O., Miller, R. I., and Williford, A. M. "The Role, Scope, and Function of the Chief Academic Affairs Officer." Paper presented at the 27th annual meeting of the Association for Institutional Research Conference, Kansas City, Mo., May 1987.

Moore, C. W. *The Mediation Process: Practical Strategies for Resolving Conflict.* San Francisco: Jossey-Bass, 1986.

Munitz, B. "Examining Administrative Performance." In P. Jedamus, M. W. Peterson, and Associates, *Improving Academic Management: A Handbook of Planning and Institutional Research.* San Francisco: Jossey-Bass, 1980.

National Association of Student Personnel Administrators. *A Perspective on Student Affairs.* Washington, D.C.: National Association of Student Personnel Administrators, 1987.

National Association of Student Personnel Administrators. *Membership Directory.* Washington, D.C.: National Association of Student Personnel Administrators, 1989.

National Governors' Association. *Time for Results: The Governor's 1991 Report on Education.* Washington, D.C.: National Governors' Association, 1986.

National Institute of Education. *Involvement in Learning: Realizing the Potential of American Higher Education.* Washington, D.C.: National Institute of Education, 1984.

Newcomb, T. M. *College Peer Groups.* Chicago: Aldine, 1966.

Noel, L., Levitz, R., Saluri, D., and Associates. *Increasing Student Retention: Effective Programs and Practices for Reducing the Dropout Rate.* San Francisco: Jossey-Bass, 1985.

Ostroth, D. D., Efird, F. D., and Lerman, L. S. "Career Patterns of Chief Student Affairs Officers." *Journal of College Student Personnel,* 1984, *25,* 443–447.

Peters, T. J., and Waterman, R. H. *In Search of Excellence: Les-*

sons from America's Best-Run Companies. New York: Harper & Row, 1982.

Powers, D. R., and Powers, M. F. *Making Participatory Management Work: Leadership of Consultive Decision Making in Academic Administration.* San Francisco: Jossey-Bass, 1983.

Pray, F. C. (ed.). *Handbook for Educational Fund Raising: A Guide to Successful Principles and Practices for Colleges, Universities, and Schools.* San Francisco: Jossey-Bass, 1981.

Rickard, S. T. "Career Pathways of Chief Student Affairs Officers: Making Room at the Top for Females and Minorities." *NASPA Journal,* 1985, *22,* 52–60.

Rodgers, R. F. "Theories Underlying Student Development." In D. G. Creamer (ed.), *Student Development in Higher Education: Theories, Practices, and Future Directions.* Cincinnati, Ohio: American College Personnel Association Media, 1980.

Rowland, A. W. *Handbook of Institutional Advancement: A Modern Guide to Executive Management, Institutional Relations, Fund Raising, Alumni Administration, Government Relations, Publications, Periodicals, and Enrollment Management.* San Francisco: Jossey-Bass, 1986.

Rudolph, F. *The American College and University: A History.* New York: Vintage Books, 1965.

Sandeen, A. *Undergraduate Education: Conflict and Change.* Lexington, Mass.: Heath, 1976.

Schlossberg, N. K., Lynch, A. Q., and Chickering, A. W. *Improving Higher Education Environments for Adults: Responsive Programs and Services from Entry to Departure.* San Francisco: Jossey-Bass, 1989.

Seldin, P. *Evaluating and Developing Administrative Performance: A Practical Guide for Academic Leaders.* San Francisco: Jossey-Bass, 1988.

Stodt, M. M., and Klepper, W. M. (eds.). *Increasing Retention: Academic and Student Affairs Administrators in Partnership.* New Directions for Higher Education, no. 60. San Francisco: Jossey-Bass, 1987.

Ury, W. L., Brett, J. M., and Goldberg, S. B. *Getting Disputes Resolved: Designing Systems to Cut the Costs of Conflict.* San Francisco: Jossey-Bass, 1988.

Varney, G. H. *Building Productive Teams: An Action Guide and Resource Book.* San Francisco: Jossey-Bass, 1989.

Walker, D. E. *The Effective Administrator: A Practical Approach to Problem Solving, Decision Making, and Campus Leadership.* San Francisco: Jossey-Bass, 1979.

Wilshire, B. *The Moral Collapse of the University: Professionalism, Purity, and Alienation.* Ithaca: State University of New York Press, 1989.

Wilson, W. "The Spirit of Learning." In *Selected Literary and Political Papers and Addresses of Woodrow Wilson.* New York: Grosset & Dunlap, 1925.

Withey, S. B. *A Degree and What Else?* New York: McGraw-Hill, 1971.

Yates, D., Jr. *The Politics of Management: Exploring the Inner Workings of Public and Private Organizations.* San Francisco: Jossey-Bass, 1985.

INDEX